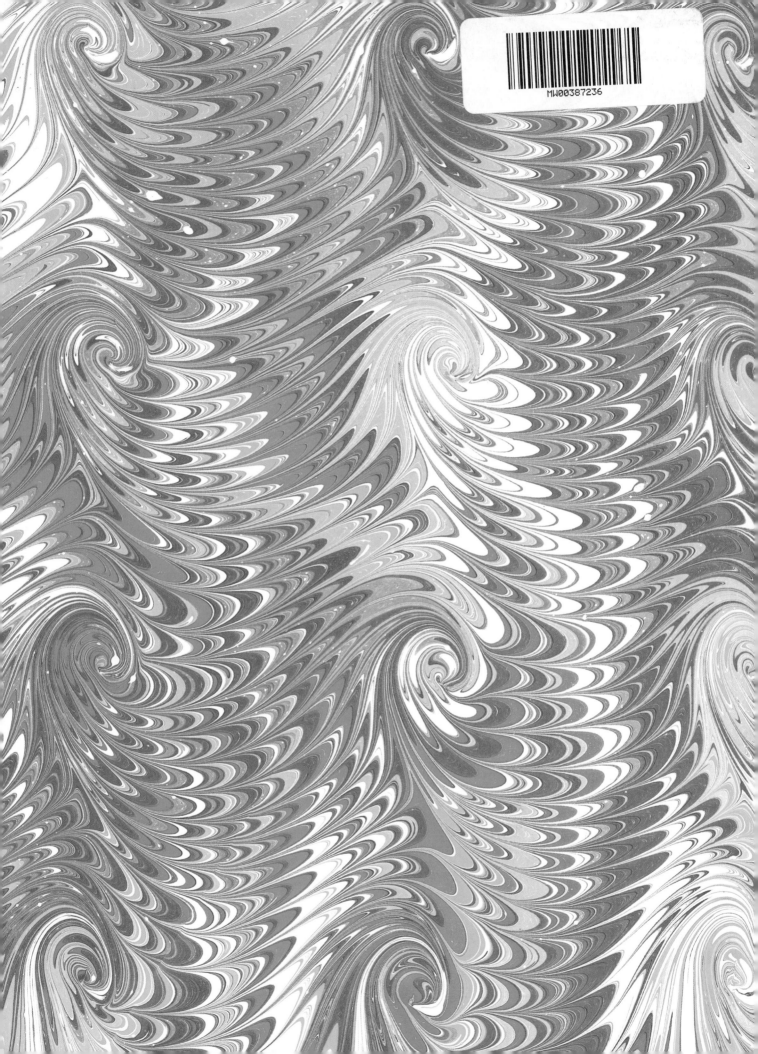

Moss Lamps

Lighting The '50s

Schiffer Publishing Ltd

4880 Lower Valley Road, Atglen, PA 19310 USA

Text By Donald-Brian Johnson

Photography & Design By Leslie Piña

DEDICATION

For Teresa and Doug Becker, and for Genevieve, Lindsy, and Nate, who like "the lamps that spin".

Layout by Bonnie M. Hensley
Type set in BernhardMod BT/Korinna BT

ISBN: 0-7643-1002-X
Printed in China
1 2 3 4

Published by Schiffer Publishing Ltd.
4880 Lower Valley Road
Atglen, PA 19310
Phone: (610) 593-1777; Fax: (610) 593-2002
E-mail: Schifferbk@aol.com
Please visit our website catalog at **www.schifferbooks.com**

In Europe, Schiffer books are distributed by Bushwood Books
6 Marksbury Avenue Kew Gardens
Surrey TW9 4JF England
Phone: 44 (0)181 392-8585; Fax: 44 (0)181 392-9876
E-mail: Bushwd@aol.com

This book may be purchased from the publisher.
Include $3.95 for shipping. Please try your bookstore first.
We are interested in hearing from authors with book ideas on related subjects.
You may write for a free printed catalog.

CONTENTS

ACKNOWLEDGMENTS

Our sincere appreciation to the Moss family, whose memories and lifetime of work made this book possible. Special thanks, for hospitality and a wealth of Moss-related information, are due family members Jay Benjamin, Jori Slater Benjamin, Carol Moss Goodstein, Stan Goodstein, Jerry Slater, and, of course, the one and only Thelma Moss, whose personality continues to outshine every Moss lamp!

Our thanks also to former Moss employees Carlos Calonje, John Disney, Beulah Rasmussen, and Yolanda Pleitez for their insights, and to Moss business associate Sid Bass for sharing his recollections with us.

Archival photos in *Moss Lamps: Lighting the '50s* are courtesy of the Thelma Moss Trust. However, the following Moss collectors provided many of our colorful examples of Moss lamps, and we are grateful for their generosity: Jeff Bukas (773) 486-3737; Joe Anthony and Marie Christine Londrico (330) 764-4058, 524 S. Court Street, Medina, OH 44256; William J. Burke; Richard A. Elioff; Brenda Jackson Boyd; David Meyer, Pleasure to Measure Custom Sewing, Eureka Springs, AR; Ken Paruti; and Amy Paliwoda. Photos of the Bukas and Londrico collections, as well as all copywork photos of archival materials, are by Leslie Piña. On-site photos were taken by Donald-Brian Johnson; all additional object photos have been supplied by the Moss collectors.

Others whose contributions to *Moss Lamps* we gratefully acknowledge include: Blue Flamingo; Denis Christiansen and Alan Trickett; Cope Plastics, Inc.; Bill Coppock; Barbara Endter; Cheryl M. Gorski; Bob Grimes; Tim Holthaus and Jim Petzold, Ceramic Arts Studio Collectors Association; Dennis Carl Hopp; Heather Jeche; Meshell Jesse, 20/60 Modern; Charles M. Johnson, Sr. and Patricia P. Johnson; Hank Kuhlmann; Modernaires 20th Century Design; Paula Ockner; Office Depot Omaha; Ramón Piña; Seelye Plastics, Inc.; John and Donna Thorpe; and as always, Peter Schiffer, Jennifer Lindbeck, Bonnie Hensley, and all the staff at Schiffer Publishing. Thanks to all, for helping make *Moss Lamps: Lighting the '50s* an "electrifying" experience!

Thelma Moss, Gerry Moss, and that lovable mascot of Moss Manufacturing, Terry the poodle. Here, Terry seems to be getting a lecture on the perils of selling lamps below cost!

FOREWORD

I first met Mr. and Mrs. Moss in 1987, while dating their granddaughter Jori, now my wife. The Mosses were working six days a week and enjoying their retail store, the Moss Lighting Company, which was one block away from the original Moss Manufacturing plant where the Moss lamps were produced. After Mr. Moss' death in 1992, Jori and I spent weekends and occasional days visiting and assisting Mrs. Moss in her various enterprises. Eventually, this became a full-time career.

At that time, I had no idea what Moss lamps looked like. The Mosses were constantly updating their lives and their business; as such, "those old things" were discarded, and virtually none of their famous lamps remained. However, when Mr. Moss purchased the building at 1026 Mission Street, some manufacturing did continue on the third floor, until the retail business took over. Eventually this area became the repair department. I always found the remaining boxes of ceramic, brass decorations, wild lampshade trim, and various lamp parts interesting, but had no way of knowing how they all came together. It was only in the last year of business, while cleaning up this third floor warehouse, that I found original inventory photographs in a box behind a paint booth. Frequent calls from collectors for the motors and various parts piqued my interest in the history of the products. By the time Donald-Brian Johnson contacted us about writing a book on Moss, we had acquired several of the lamps, and become collectors ourselves.

Gerry Moss attributed the company's success to "good luck and good people", particu-larly John Disney and Duke Smith. Mr. and Mrs. Moss were dedicated to each other and to their business; they had a total commitment to what they did. I can only imagine the constant redesigning that was required before each product was finally approved. That attention to detail is what makes the Moss lamps unique. When you see a room full of these lamps and their figurines, you are in the presence of the Mosses. The lamps reflect their personal style and sense of humor.

Moss lamps are true classics. So are Gerry and Thelma Moss.

Jay Benjamin
The Thelma Moss Trust

San Francisco, California
April, 1999

The sign that welcomed visitors to Moss Lighting, 1026 Mission Street, San Francisco, California.

INTRODUCTION

Modern. . .is an expression of attitudes toward living, and cannot be the same for everyone.

Edward J. Wormley
Dunbar Book of Modern Furniture

I found my first Moss lamp at an Omaha garage sale. Not at an antique shop, collectibles show, estate sale, or anywhere remotely grand, but at an old-fashioned, clean-out-the-house-from-attic-to-cellar garage sale. In a garage. In Omaha.

That rainy spring day, I spotted the sign first—"Sale Today"—hand-lettered on cardboard and posted crookedly next to an open, one-car garage. Then I saw *the lamp*. Before I knew it, my car had coasted to the curb, and I was inside the garage for a better look.

I'd never seen anything like it: white and black plastic pieces (now that we've formalized the relationship, it's "plexiglas") stuck together in an

An Omaha garage sale find: #2310 for just $30! 5' h. *Johnson collection*

odd, but oddly appealing blend of curves and angles. There was a planter below, and, on a platform above, perched a serene ceramic gentleman in vaguely oriental costume. The shade, while probably not authentic, looked right for the period. Wow!

"It lights up, you know." Well, I'd figured that. After all, it was a lamp. The garage sale entrepreneur, seeing my puzzled expression, continued. "No, I mean this part lights up". He flipped a switch. "And this part, too". Another switch, and suddenly the small plexiglas cubicles above and below the serene ceramic man were alight. "He even used to rotate—you know, spin around—but he doesn't anymore. Just makes this terrible whirring noise."

Rotate? Spin? Forget the 'terrible whirring noise'. "How much?"

He thought about it for a moment. "Well, it was my mother-in-law's, and actually I hate the thing—the lamp, not my mother-in-law. How's $30 sound?"

It must have sounded fine, because the next thing I recall is trying to figure out how to stow a floor lamp in a Jeep. (Hint: remove the shade and figurine first.) Thus began my introduction to the world of Moss lamps.

Actually, for the longest time, I didn't know that I *had* a Moss lamp, or even what a Moss lamp was. One day, with

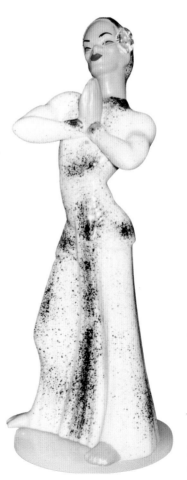

Detail, #2310 figurine. "Mr. Mambo" by Decoramic Kilns.

nothing better to do, I decided to see if there was some way of getting the spin function going again. (The previous owner was right: it didn't work, and it did make a whirring noise.) I laid the lamp on its side to check the wiring, and there, on the inside of the plexiglas base, I saw a stamp: *"Copyrighted Moss Mfg. Co. San Francisco, Calif."* Hmmmm. Never heard of them. And I still couldn't get that motor to work.

As luck would have it, soon after I was speaking with my friend Dennis Carl Hopp, a knowledgeable dealer in mid-twentieth century artifacts. I asked if he had any information on "Moss Manufacturing", as I seemed to be in possession of one of their lamps.

"You have a Moss lamp? Well, they're really something special. And quite collectible, too. How much did you pay?" I told him. Silence, then: ". . .and you got an awfully good deal!"

Dennis was right. I did get a good deal. (Omaha garage sellers are now forewarned.) I also got something more: an abiding interest in learning more about the company that made "the lamps that spin".

My next bit of information came courtesy of Bob Grimes, noted sheet music collector and long-time San Franciscan. During one of our phone conversations, I asked if he knew of a San Francisco company called Moss Manufacturing—a company that made lamps.

"Moss? Why, yes. But I don't think they make lamps anymore. They're into real estate and things. In fact, I live in a Moss apartment building. Do you want their phone number?"

I did, and I got it, and so one thing led to another. My call to Moss Properties put me in touch with Jay Benjamin, grandson-in-law of Thelma and Gerry Moss and representative for the Thelma Moss Trust. I asked *the question:*

"Plexiglas lamps? Well, Moss hasn't made those since—oh, I guess the late '60s." (Disappointed silence from my end of the line.) "And, since Mrs. Moss retired last year, we've closed the Moss Lighting showroom. We're liquidating what's left before we sell the building." (More disappointment.) "But right now, the third floor workroom is just as it was back when they were making the lamps—all the parts and equipment are still in place." (Hope rises anew.) "I could probably locate some old files and inventory photos for you, give you a tour, get some of the staff and family together . . . and of course you could meet Mrs. Moss." (Bingo!)

I called my co-author Leslie Piña, with news of my Moss detective work thus far. "You know Leslie, I think we might have a good book here."

"Wrong, Don," she replied. I *know* we have a good book here!

Well, we'll leave the final decision up to you. But we're confident you'll find this genial story of "the lamps that spin" and the people who created them as fascinating as we have. While "modern cannot be the same for everyone", we hope that, for the here and now, modern for *you* is the world of Moss lamps.

(Incidentally, Jay Benjamin did manage to dig a "brand new 1950s motor" out of storage for me before the Moss building closed for good in 1998. My #2310 Moss lamp spins perfectly now, thank you, and the figurine, "Mr. Mambo", no longer makes that terrible whirring noise.)

Moss family members and staff gather in San Francisco, to reminisce about the heyday of Moss Lighting and Manufacturing. *Front:* Carlos Calonje, master electrician, involved in all aspects of Moss lamp production; Beulah Rasmussen, sales associate, and longtime personal friend of Thelma Moss. *Center:* Moss Lamps: Lighting the '50s co-author Donald-Brian Johnson; Moss son-in-law, and former company sales representative and factory manager, Stan Goodstein; Moss granddaughter Jori Slater Benjamin; grandson-in-law Jay Benjamin, representative for the Thelma Moss Trust. *Back:* office worker Yolanda Pleitez; Carol Moss Goodstein, daughter of Thelma and Gerry Moss, and a former Moss employee; Jerry Slater, Moss son-in-law, and former plant and general manager.

Part I
"Lighting the Way:
The Heyday of Moss Manufacturing"

CHAPTER 1
"LIGHTS UP: A BRIEF MOSS HISTORY"

I don't know what it was, exactly. They just had a style about them.

Beulah Rasmussen,
longtime Moss friend and employee

They certainly did. And, when the laid-back, but rock-solid business sense of Gerry Moss collided head-on with the dynamic enthusiasm of Thelma Isaacs, the result was the creative explosion we know as Moss lamps.

First Light

Gerald ("Gerry") Moss grew up in the vicinity of Puget Sound, which inspired his lifelong love of the sea. Beginning as a lamp wholesaler, he became a lamp manufacturer out of necessity. The wholesaling business burnt down, and the choices were simple: go into manufacturing or go out of business.

Thelma ("Thel") Isaacs was a second-generation Californian and a businesswoman before it was fashionable to be one. Her successful venture into the field of women's ready-to-wear clothes eventually encompassed ownership of sixteen Mode O'Day stores throughout California.

Thelma and Gerry met in a way that usually only happens in the movies. Both attended a party, Gerry with another date. He saw Thelma "across a crowded room", introduced himself, and ended up giving her a ride home. The couple married in the early 1930s and kept busy with their separate professional interests: Thelma with Mode O'Day and Gerry with the beginnings of Moss Manufacturing.

The Moss company started up production in 1937. The lamps of those early years were far different than the plexiglas models Moss later became famous for. These were traditional metal-stemmed lamps with fabric shades—functional, unobtrusive, and just what a still-Depression-strapped public wanted. Moss Manufacturing flourished not only through sales to furniture stores, but also as the largest supplier of traditional lamps for Sears Roebuck & Co.

Uncle Sam Wants Steel!

Then, World War II intervened. Materials were rationed, and steel was necessary for the war effort, with no surplus available for such home front frivolities as lamps. Moss Manufacturing secured a government contract for the construction of mine detonators and, in return, was permitted a certain number of days per month, and hours per day, for lamp production.

So, lamps could be made—but out of what? With steel unavailable in sufficient quantities, thoughts turned to other possibilities. Something modern. Something easy to assemble. And something no one else was using. Finally, Moss designer Duke Smith came up with the answer: plexiglas!

Plexiglas (dubbed "plastic" in the Moss literature) is the trade name for an acrylic product developed by the Rohm & Haas company in 1934. While today's collectors interchangeably use the terms plastic, plexiglas, acrylic, and lucite to describe the material that constitutes a Moss lamp, plexiglas is the most accurate one. Rohm & Haas probably never envisioned their product as a medium for lamp construction, but they had no reason to complain: by the early 1950s, Moss Manufacturing was the largest user of Rohm & Haas plexiglas in the United States.

When the Lights Went on Again

With the end of World War II, the fresh look of Moss lamps sparked the interest of a buying public ready to make up for the austerity of the war years. Plexiglas lamps, an idea born of necessity, became the key to Moss Manufacturing's success. Duke Smith's designs are a hallmark of those early years: non-figural lamps, with angular plexi pieces arranged in sharply defined linear configurations. Then, with the dawn of the 1950s, came three arrivals that prominently figured into Moss' soon-to-be-greater-than-ever success: Thelma Moss, John Disney . . . and the revolving figurine.

Lightning Strikes!

Ladies first: By 1950, Thelma Moss was firmly established in her Mode O'Day proprietorship, but Gerry Moss, always on the lookout for new ideas, determined that the new ideas Moss Manufacturing needed were Thelma's. Somewhat reluctantly, she was persuaded to give up her involvement with Mode O'Day and combine her business and design talents with Gerry's aptitude for management and sales.

At almost the same time, extraordinary designer John Disney became a part of the Moss team. Former employees agree that an electric current of creativity linked John Disney and Thelma Moss. "Between him and Thel", says former plant and general manager Jerry Slater, "they did almost all of it. He'd do all the mechanics, she'd come up with ideas and change things." Adds Stan Goodstein, the company's former sales representative and factory manager, "John would draw up a lot of sketches, and then they would work together and pick out the ones that they liked." But all agree it was a joint creative effort. "John was very, very good at why he did," says Beulah Rasmussen, "and Thelma initiated many of the main ideas. Her mind could go in one hundred different directions at the same time!"

A major idea all credit to John Disney is the introduction of the Moss revolve platform, with its the familiar spinning figures. Utilizing the electrical abilities of Carlos Calonje and the plexi-cutting wizardry of, among others, Cliff Routley, the Moss "lamps that spin" took Moss Manufacturing's popularity to dazzling new heights. Soon, *The Price Is Right* was giving away Moss lamps as contestant prizes, . . . celebrity guests on the early California TV program *Stairway to Stardom* were treated to complimentary Moss plexiglas lighters, . . . and Gerry Moss was finally able to indulge his boyhood passion for the sea as skipper of the *Thelma I* and her eventual successors.

Top right: Lavish promotional card for Moss Lighting. "Without exaggeration, over 500 chandeliers on display."

Bottom right: Main office, Moss Manufacturing, 1124 Mission Street, San Francisco.

10

Who Bought What, & Where, & Why

Gerry Moss was very innovative—he wasn't afraid to try things. Those lamps were totally different from what people were used to. In fact, when they first came out, we laughed and said "that isn't going to go". But we were wrong. Moss kept bringing out new things, and did very well.

Sid Bass
former sales representative,
Rembrandt Lamps

Moss lamps weren't marketed to the individual consumer, which is why so few examples of period company advertising exist. Instead, new Moss models were introduced to furniture dealers around the country at "market time"—the huge display shows held each year in such major metro locations as San Francisco, Los Angeles, Seattle, Chicago, Dallas, Toronto, New York, and Boston. Competition for customers at the market shows was fierce, and manufacturers, Moss among them, were notably secretive about their new releases. Sid Bass recalls that before a show opened, Moss would "cover their windows, so people wouldn't look in and see the new stuff." Once the show was underway, Bass notes that Moss would "place their most interesting new items right up front. Our Rembrandt showroom across the way was a big draw, and Gerry made sure the traffic flow of customers stopped at Moss, too!" Amidst this friendly rivalry, furniture dealers would place orders for "the latest" from Moss; after the show, enough lamps to

Thelma Moss (*right*) and friend model party hats that would be right at home atop a Moss lamp.

Gerry Moss, on the flying bridge of the *Thelma IV.*

Thelma and Gerry Moss enjoy a gala evening out. (The gentleman in the back seems to have arrived bearing gifts!)

fill those orders would be produced. If a prototype failed to attract buyers, it remained a prototype (or, with some revision, re-emerged as an entry at the next market show).

An average-sized furniture store such as Helsley in Napa, or Deovlet & Sons in San Francisco, might order perhaps four or five pairs of Moss lamps at a time. A larger firm, such as Chicago's Polk Brothers might expand their order to an even dozen. Naturally, exclusive firms at the high end of the buying spectrum, supplying lamps to interior decorators as well as to individual consumers, were prime Moss clientele. But interestingly enough, there was also a steady market for Moss lamps among the "3 rooms for $99" stores, those outlets seeking upscale accent items to deflect attention from their otherwise "discount" inventory. Even among furnishings disparagingly referred to as "Bronx Renaissance", Moss products stood out as, in the words of one salesman, "the best of the borax". Upscale or down, the Moss customer base was never middle of the road!

Although nearly one thousand lamp and other plexiglas designs were introduced during the lifetime of Moss Manufacturing, only 5 to 10 percent account for the major portion of the company's revenue. Leading the way was #T459 and its matching floor lamp, #2293. "We used to call them the 'Leaning Lenas'", says Carol Moss Goodstein, "because of the way they leaned! With those fluorescent tubes in the middle, they were our best sellers".

The Light Fades

Original inventory photos, some with "X's" across the image, others carrying handwritten notations, indicate that as the '50s waned, so did interest in Moss plexi. Many slower-selling items, such as smokestands and the more austere floor lamps, were phased out, with major line reductions occurring in 1959. Some stalwarts of the early years, such as aquarium tables, "leaf lamps", and the popular revolving figurals, still soldiered on into the '60s, but tastes were changing, and sales dwindling.

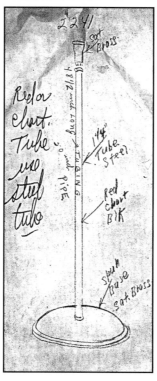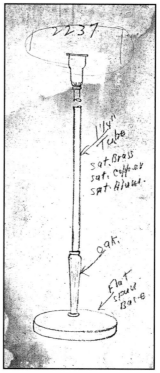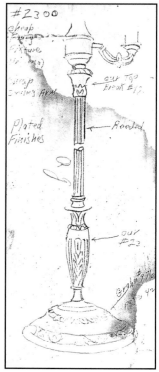

Top: A Moss showroom window of the early 1940s, featuring traditional Moss styles that predate the plexiglas lamps. The promotional flyer reads *"Moss Lamps: Styled Right For Better Light"*.

Bottom left: Design sketch for an early traditional Moss floor lamp, #2241.

Bottom center: Another traditional lamp sketch, #2237.

Bottom right: And a third, #2300. (As "cheap" is mentioned several times in the accompanying assembly notes, it's a safe bet this fixture was not at the top of the Moss line!)

When production ceased in 1968, the most recent best-sellers were the less adventurous, ceramic-based "Tami" lamps: certainly attractive, but less challenging to the home decor.

And so, one chapter ended and another began, as Moss Manufacturing, producer, became Moss Lighting, distributor. A leading light in modern design had been extinguished . . . but the afterglow remained.

Above: Checking out the finer points of #X 2400.

Left: A restored version of #X 2400, as found in a Wisconsin antique mall in 1998.

Top left: Gerry Moss, situated amidst the splendor of the Moss showroom.

Bottom left: In living color, #XT 800, the lamp Mr. Moss is holding in the above photo, and its partner. Base only, 1' h. *Courtesy of Joe Anthony and Marie Christine Londrico*

13

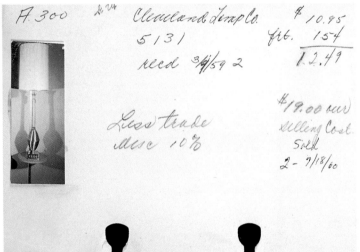

Top left: An original Moss invoice dating from 1947. The penciled note at the bottom advises, "please ship above as soon as convenient, as customer has modern living room sets coming and *no modern lamps!*"

Top right: Another early Moss invoice, this one for Sears Roebuck & Co., noting that "Mr. Moss will select shades."

Bottom left: In later years, Moss also served as a sales center for lamps produced by other manufacturers. This card, from 1959, depicts a Cleveland Lamp Co. product distributed by Moss.

Bottom right: Moss Lighting business card.

Panelists on the early California television program *Stairway to Stardom* were delighted to receive Moss lighters as one of the perks of participation. Shown with Gerry Moss and host Dennis James are several stars who had already climbed that stairway. *From left:* Louis Da Pron, Hilo Hattie, Fifi D'Orsay, and Ted Lesser.

Dennis and four more glittering names of a bygone era. *From left:* Helen Parrish, David Rose, Louise Beavers, and, back for another lighter, Ted Lesser.

And the stars never cease! *From left:* Phil Regan, Lois Collier, Dennis James, Rudy Vallee, and—guess who—Ted Lesser! (*Stairway to Stardom's* sponsor was Crest. It's probably not coincidental that the tiny crowns on the "Crest Ballots" resemble toothbrushes.)

Ted Lesser must be on his lunch break. Here, Dennis James watches as Freddy Martin and Preston Sturges somewhat gingerly examine their Moss lighters. (Incidentally, no one went home empty-handed; *Stairway to Stardom* contestants all received Moss lighters too.)

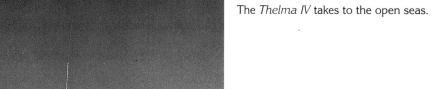

The *Thelma IV* takes to the open seas.

Gerry Moss, in the wheelhouse of the *Thelma IV*.

Thelma Moss christens a cruiser.

The Moss-designed clock/barometer from the *Thelma IV*.

Gerry, Carol, and Thelma Moss enjoy all the comforts of home aboard ship (including a selection of Moss lighters on the coffee table).

The *Thelma IV* was roomy; as Thelma Moss noted in a yachting publication interview, "even with guests we're not crowded". Adding a bit of late-1950s star-power are two such Moss guests: Barbara Eden (pre-*I Dream Of Jeannie*) and her then-husband, Michael Ansara, star of *Broken Arrow*.

A frisky pose from Barbara. All that fresh sea air can be invigorating!

Top: A longtime member of the Moss staff, and the man responsible for working out the electrical intricacies of the Moss lamps, Carlos Calonje.

Bottom: An "18th and 16th birthday celebration". Mrs. Moss with good friend Beulah Rasmussen, a member of the Moss sales staff for many years, in 1996.

Moss family and friends gather on board the *Thelma IV*. Gerry and Thelma's other daughter, Marilyn, is at far left.

CHAPTER 2
"LET THERE BE LIGHT: THE MAKING OF A MOSS LAMP"

I remember gluing all those pictures in all those books.
Carol Moss Goodstein

Those "books" were the secret ingredient behind the superior construction of every Moss lamp. As each prototype was completed, it was carefully photographed, the photo glued in a notebook, and reference notations entered on the page, or on the photo itself. Since Moss Manufacturing relied on hand, rather than automated assembly, the job of each of the 20 to 30 Moss employees required 100 percent accuracy. With a notebook entry as guide, quality control and precision were assured at every stage of lamp production.

But let's begin at the beginning, in the words of those who were there. It always started with a sketch . . .

Design

STAN GOODSTEIN: "Duke Smith, and later John Disney, would present some designs to Thel; they'd discuss what they liked and make a decision. John enhanced what Duke was doing. What Duke wanted was simplicity in production. John got into the more elaborate versions, which were of course harder to put together."

JERRY SLATER: "When Duke was there, he had two base designs, so the bases would be the same for production purposes, and then they'd put these different backgrounds on the bases. When John Disney came in, he got more elaborate and every one was different.

After the design was approved, John would get together with Cliff Routley, and they'd figure out how to make it work, so the first samples could be made. Cliff would say, 'we can't do it, this just won't work.' And John would reply, 'well, we'll *find* a way to make it work.' Plexiglas lamps were very labor intensive, and there were new models twice a year, with at least 30 new ones annually."

Working with Plexi

JERRY SLATER: "Working with plexiglas, it was tough to sand the angles, or to drill them, so I got an idea. I

had a 'Shopsmith' in my garage that I'd just gotten. You could fix it as a drill or a sander or a lathe, because the bed tilted both ways and so did the disk. I took it over to the factory one night to see if it would help with the plexiglas, and it did. That became a very valuable piece of equipment for us—the old 'Shopsmith'."

CARLOS CALONJE: "Plexiglas came in lots of nice colors: clear, blue, black, white, pink . . . maybe gold."

Assembly

JERRY SLATER: "You'd assemble 100 at a time on the tables, because you'd already have cut out all the bases and all the parts. Then you'd just put them all together individually; it was all just bench work. I used to figure costs, and I estimate it took maybe two days to do 100 lamps, because you had six guys working on them doing different parts. We could do maybe 250 a week, 1000 a month.

One of the main tools we used was the eyedropper. We used to buy eyedroppers by the ton, for applying cement to put the pieces together. Today they'd probably use a syringe or something, but in those days it was the eyedropper."

CARLOS CALONJE: "We'd heat the eyedropper with a blow torch so it came to a thin point. We'd pull it up and make it very fine. You'd glue the bases together and then you'd glue the other parts, and then you'd have to stick on the back. And then each one had to be wired differently."

Shades

JERRY SLATER: "Girls made the shades in a different room. The spun glass itself was just like the kind you see today at Christmas. Not fiberglass—that was smoother. The formula that saturated the spun glass, well it was kind of a secret how to mix that up; a lot of people tried and couldn't do it. The ingredients all came from different suppliers, and only Moss knew how to combine them. This mixture made the spun glass adhere and gave it a hard shell. We had these 55-gallon

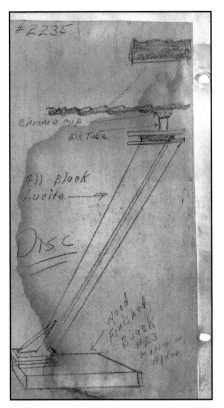

It all starts with a sketch. Shown is the original design for floor lamp #2235.

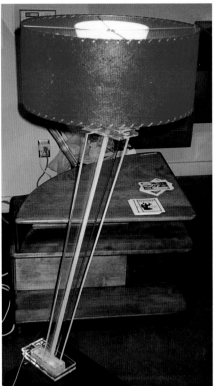

And the finished product! The clear plexiglas is an alternate to the "black lucite" specified on the #2235 sketch. The shade, while period, is not original. *Courtesy of Modernaires 20th Century Design*

Add up the parts, add up the labor, figure the expenses, and arrive at a selling price. The cost of each new addition to the Moss line was calculated on a pricing worksheet such as this.

PLASTIC TABLE OR FLOOR LAMP NO						
MATERIAL						
	Color					
1/8" Plexi		sq. in		@		per in
3/16" "		sq. in		@		per in
1/4" "		sq. in		@		per in
3/8" "		sq. in		@		per in
1/2" "		sq. in		@		per in
1" "		sq. in		@		per in
P.5 "		sq. in		@		per in
Corr "		sq. in		@		per in
3/8" Rod Clear		in		@		per in
1/2" Rod Clear		in		@		per in
3/4" Rod Clear		in		@		per in
	Color					
3/4" Tubing		in		@		per in
1" Tubing		in		@		per in
2" Tubing		in		@		per in

LABOR

Cutting time _____ @ _____ per _____

Assembly time _____ @ _____ per _____

Miscellaneous Material or Labor

Remarks

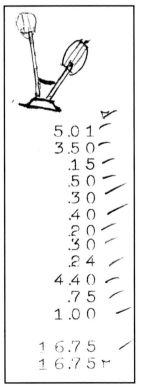

Here, the costs of table lamp #T 687 have been tabulated on a bit of adding machine tape that also includes the design sketch! Total cost of manufacture was $16.75 (parts $12.50, labor $4.25).

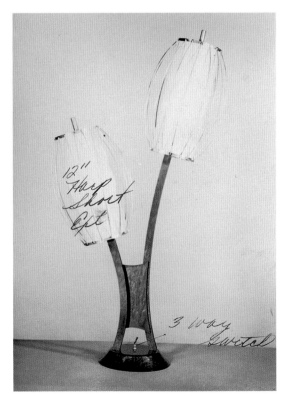

Original inventory photo of # T 687.

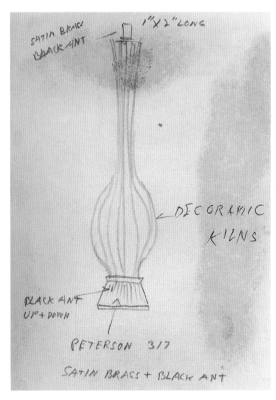

Design sketch for Tami lamp # 54 A

19

The eight photos that follow are designer renditions of smoking stands in the early Moss "traditional" style, predating the introduction of plexiglas.

Top: #4616, #4618

Center: *(from left)* #4626, #4619, #4620

Bottom: *(from left)* #4621, #4622, #4623

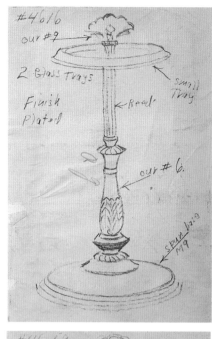

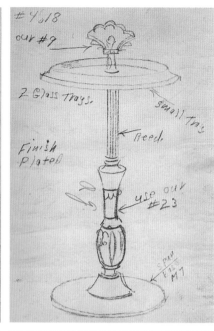

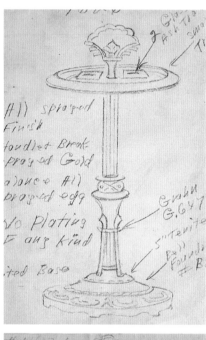

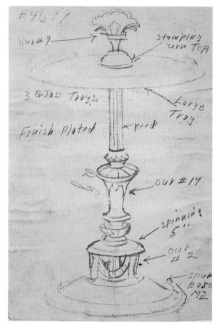

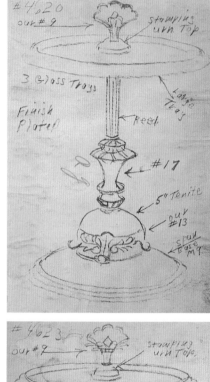

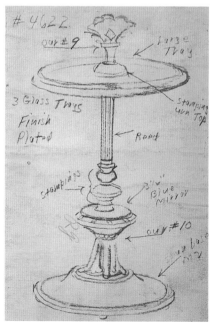

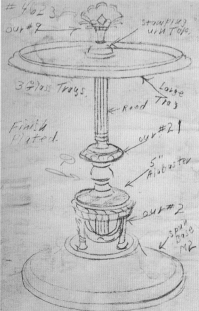

drums, and we'd just mix it right in the drums. We called the stuff 'tish'.

The girls would place the spun glass in sheet metal shade molds and brush on the 'tish'. Then each filled mold would cure overnight. The next day, they'd use an extended shoehorn to break the seal between the mold and the shade. The shades would pop right out like cookies from a pan."

CAROL MOSS GOODSTEIN: "Did you know the original shade color was white? It's age that's discolored them. There were other shade materials, too: fabric, 'skin', some parchment. And the same shade would show up on several different models."

Shipping

JERRY SLATER: "Packing these for shipping was a problem all by itself. They'd be shipped in shredded paper, with figurines and finials wrapped, and the shades were shipped separately. Often, we even sent along assembly instructions. But there was still some damage."

Top center: No plexiglas yet, but a more recognizably "modern" Moss look. Smoking stand #4624.

Top right: #4625

Center: Plexiglas at last! Smoking stand #4627.

Center right: The perfect complement to a Moss lamp of the '50s: smoking stand #4628.

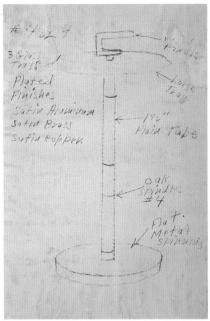

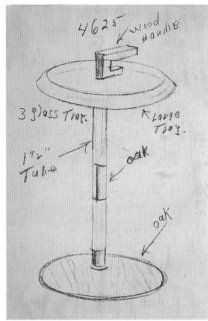

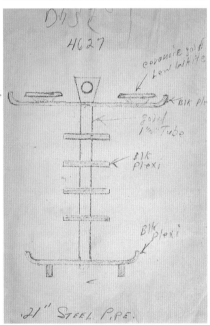

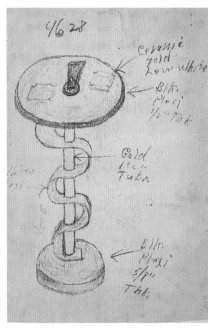

Samples of Rohm and Haas plexiglas from the Moss workshop.

Moss' plexiglas supplier of choice, Rohm & Haas, introduced the clear thermoplastic compound in 1934. At one time, Moss was the largest user of Rohm and Haas plexiglas in the United States.

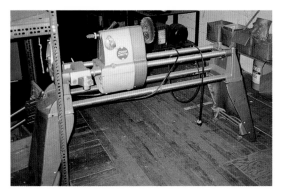

The little machine that made it all possible: a home "Shopsmith", transported to the Moss factory, meant plexiglas could be cut in any shape the designer envisioned.

Metal background components, often included in a Moss lamp design.

Here's what makes the world go 'round—or at least the figurines! One of the tiny motors responsible for the revolve function on many Moss lamps, stamped with the Moss logo. (Another motor, similar in size, required a slightly different attachment to the lamp base.)

The underpinnings of a Moss lamp. Connecting wires are concealed inside the metal box, and the Moss copyright trademark is visible at left, stamped on the plexiglas.

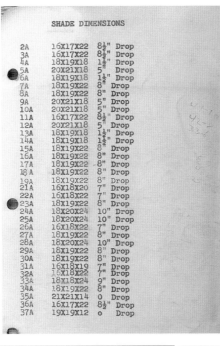

SHADE DIMENSIONS

2A	16X17X22	8½"	Drop
3A	16X17X22	8½"	Drop
4A	18X19X18	1½"	Drop
5A	20X21X18	5"	Drop
6A	18X19X18	1½"	Drop
7A	18X19X22	8"	Drop
8A	18X19X22	8"	Drop
9A	20X21X18	5"	Drop
10A	20X21X18	5"	Drop
11A	16X17X22	8½"	Drop
12A	20X21X18	5"	Drop
13A	18X19X18	1½"	Drop
14A	18X19X18	1½"	Drop
15A	18X19X22	8"	Drop
16A	18X19X22	8"	Drop
17A	18X19X22	8"	Drop
18A	18X19X22	8"	Drop
19A	18X19X22	8"	Drop
21A	16X18X20	7"	Drop
22A	16X18X22	7"	Drop
23A	18X19X22	8"	Drop
24A	18X20X24	10"	Drop
25A	18X20X24	10"	Drop
26A	16X18X22	7"	Drop
27A	18X19X22	8"	Drop
28A	18X20X24	10"	Drop
29A	18X19X22	8"	Drop
30A	18X19X22	8"	Drop
31A	16X18X19	7"	Drop
32A	16X18X22	7"	Drop
33A	18X18X24	9"	Drop
34A	18X19X22	8"	Drop
35A	21X21X14	0	Drop
36A	16X17X22	8½"	Drop
37A	19X19X12	o	Drop

Top left: Few original spun glass shades survive the years intact. Those that do beautifully soften the transmitted light, making repair work worth the effort. #T 740. 3' 7" h. *Photo courtesy of William J. Burke*

Top center: For speedy assembly, workers could refer to this listing of available shades and sizes.

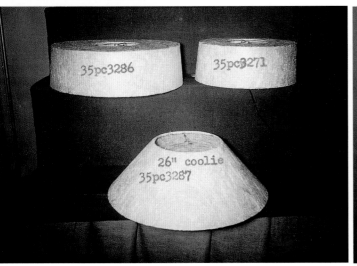

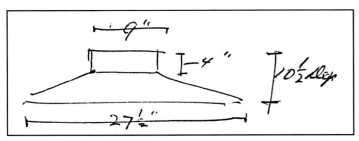

Center left: Three popular spun glass shade styles. *Front:* 26" 'coolie', #35pc3287. *Back:* #35pc3286; #35pc3271.

Center right: Four more. *Front:* #35pc3282; #35pc3281. *Back:* 20" 'coolie' #35pc3285; #35pc3284.

Bottom left: Original sketch for shade #35pc3282.

Bottom right: Shade #35pc3282 in place on floor lamp #2293, the "Leaning Lena". Over time, the "secret formula" used to cure Moss spun glass shades has darkened to a rich golden hue. Unless painted however, all original spun glass shades were *white!*

Unique curved shade. (Table lamp #T 617, featuring this shade, is shown in Chapter 8.)

Other materials were also used for shade construction, including this butterfly-patterned bamboo.

Metal trim pieces such as these were often used as decorative accents on Moss shades.

Ceramic trim accents were also popular, with a variety of options available.

Decorative braid or fringe often highlighted both spun glass and fabric shades.

Included in this ceramic trim grouping are the popular "Comedy" and "Tragedy" masks.

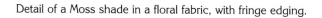
Detail of a Moss shade in a floral fabric, with fringe edging.

In this vintage promotional shot, Gerry Moss inspects the shade trim work being done by a Moss employee. The shade is model #35pc3284.

About Terry the Poodle

CAROL MOSS GOOD-STEIN: "That dog followed my mother everywhere. If she walked out in the plant, Terry would follow her there. And when Thel wasn't looking, someone would grab the air hose and tease him. My father would get such a kick out of that because Terry would just get furious. He was a very human dog."

STAN GOODSTEIN: "That dog was such a snob."

Do You Have Any Moss Lamps?

BEULAH RASMUSSEN: "*All* mine were Moss lamps. I've still got one—and it's a beauty."

Aren't they all!

Left: The ultimate in quality control: fountain lamp #T 699 is given a final inspection by Terry the poodle.

Below: The instructions say it all: "Fragile! Handle With Care!" Careful packing (and huge boxes) were always required to make certain Moss lamps arrived at their destinations in mint condition.

Diagrams were often required so workers (and recipients) would know what went where! Shown is an assembly diagram for #2365, a floor lamp with revolving figurine and three "pod" shades.

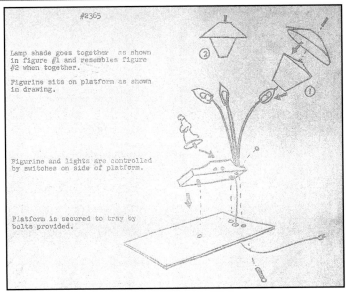

#2365

Lamp shade goes together as shown in figure #1 and resembles figure #2 when together.

Figurine sits on platform as shown in drawing.

Figurine and lights are controlled by switches on side of platform.

Platform is secured to tray by bolts provided.

MOSS LAMPS

69

FRAGILE HANDLE WITH CARE

CHAPTER 3

"FIGURATIVELY SPEAKING: THE MOSS FIGURINES"

No base. No shades. They just want the figurines.
Moss Manufacturing invoice, 1947

Moss lamps are the ideal cross-collectible. Lamp collectors like their function, '50s collectors like their design, and collectors of figurines like . . . well, you guessed it! Because many of the figures that appear on Moss lamps were produced by major ceramic design houses of the postwar period, the desirability of the lamps themselves increases. What better way to top off a Ceramic Arts Studio collection, for instance, than with a Ceramic Arts Studio Moss lamp? And, while Moss determined which figurine went with which lamp—a mix-and-match approach still favored by many of today's collectors—it's surprising just how often lamp and figure seem "made for each other".

Figuring It Out

Those firms currently accredited with figurines utilized in the Moss inventory are: *Ceramic Arts Studio, Consolidated, Decoramic Kilns, deLee Art, Dorothy Kindell, Hedi Schoop, Lefton,* and *Yona Ceramics.* Additionally, at least one lamp (#XT 812) bears a figurine signed *"The Bennetts, Caroline & Bud, CA".* However, it's not clear if "the Bennetts" were figurine designers, or just lucky recipients of a personally inscribed Moss lamp! As the blend of glazed and unglazed surfaces on #XT 812 is quite similar to that used on Consolidated's "Native Man" wall plaque, #5007, it's quite possible #XT 812 also used a Consolidated figure.

Ceramic ashtrays were a staple of the Moss line too, and again the talents of outside firms were called on. Moss smokestand ashtrays were the work of *Marvin Charles;* larger individual ashtrays (just right for placement next to a huge Moss lamp) were created by *Lyn of California Ceramics.*

Major Players: Decoramic Kilns (& Yona)

California's Decoramic Kilns provided the majority of Moss figurines, including such favorites as the "Oriental Boy and Girl", "Marilyn", and "Mambo". While Decoramic Kilns characters were often not as finely detailed as the figurines produced by better-known companies, they do have a charm and personality all their own. The sultry and aloof "Cocktail Girl", for instance, shows up on many lamps and has proven a perennial favorite with collectors. In this case, the ceramic detailing easily rivals that of figures turned out by the "name" studios.

Interestingly, Decoramic Kilns was also able to "assist" Moss in finding ways to economize on figurine costs. Says Jerry Slater, "if Moss found something they liked, they would have it copied at this ceramics place across the bay. They'd just make it a bit more schmaltzy."

The female "Bali Dancer" is a good example. On the early Moss lamps, the "Bali Dancer" figure is clearly marked "Yona Ceramics". Later, a less finely detailed version turns up in inventory photos and is then attributed to Decoramic. Examples of each on the same table lamp (#XT 831) are shown in Chapter 8. Comparison of the two indicates the Decoramic "Bali" is slightly smaller and less sharply defined, suggesting an actual Yona "Bali" figure was used to create the Decoramic mold.

Ceramic artist Yona Lippen was a former Hedi Schoop employee and a prolific Los Angeles designer. Another Yona figure, "Girl With Basket", appears on table lamp #XT 811, but so far no Decoramic double of that one has shown up!

Decoramic was also responsible for many of the incidental ceramic pieces used on Moss lamps ("Comedy and Tragedy" faces, gold balls, and the like), with *Ceramic Craft* taking up the slack. (You can check out their decorative school of butterfly fish on room divider #3501.)

Go Figure: Hedi Schoop vs. Lefton

If imitation is the highest form of flattery, then Hedi Schoop was no doubt overwhelmed to find her 1951 "Mardi Gras" figurines ("with the recognized Hedi Schoop touch") retooled and released as Lefton's 1956 "Harlequinade" pair. The "Harlequinade" boy and girl appear on many Moss designs, notably back-to-back on the popular #T 534 music box lamp. The only other documented Moss figure provided by George Zoltan Lefton Imports is the "Asian Dancer" on #XT 805.

Hedi Schoop, however, is much better represented. Although her "Mardi Gras" pair doesn't put in an appearance, the Mardi Gras-like "Dancer" steps out on several wall plaques, as well as on clock lamp #3007. Other distinctively Schoop designs used on Moss lamps include 1954's "Poodle Girl"; "Lotus Lee Fan Girl"; the beatific (and much in demand) "Phantasy Ladies," which date from the mid '50s; "Lantern Man and Woman"; and the "Young China" musician and dancer, first introduced by Schoop in 1946.

A native of Switzerland, Hedi Schoop fled Nazi Germany in the early 1930s with her husband, composer Frederick Hollander. Based in Hollywood, Hedi Schoop Art Creations specialized in decorative items, such as the figurines and figurine/planters that bring a graceful charm to the Moss lamps on which they appear. Each is very lovely—and very collectible!

All Grown Up: delee Art

Mention the name "deLee", and the mind conjures up visions of wistful ceramic skunk room deodorizers and bashful, long-lashed children. However, Jimmy Lee Stewart (Kohl), the creative talent behind the deLee name, was an artist to be reckoned with. Stewart was another Los Angeles talent, and some of her most accomplished works are her infrequent adult figures, which guest-star on Moss Lamps. Seen most often, and adding a whimsically exotic touch to every lamp they visit, are the "Siamese Man and Woman" (see #T 476 in this chapter). Also putting in verified appearances, (although not shown in *Moss Lamps*), are deLee's Hawaiian figures "Maui" and "Leilani", and a Latin dance pair. Sorry, no skunks!

The Best, from the Midwest

Moss lamps finally found their ideal figural counterparts, not on the west Coast, but in Madison, Wisconsin. These were the spectacularly dramatic figurines created by Betty Harrington for Madison's Ceramic Arts Studio, from the early 1940s through the mid-1950s. Among the most prized (and most valuable) of Moss lamps are those that carry a CAS figurine. Shown in this chapter are wall plaque #5006 with "Zor" and "Zorina", and table lamp #XT 809, with the "Water Man". Other Moss lamps with Harrington figurals that occasionally

pop up on the market are "Fire Man" and "Fire Woman" (complete with red plexiglas flames licking at their heels); "Comedy" and "Tragedy", artfully posed before plexiglas theater curtains; and the spectacularly modern "Adonis and Aphrodite", an example of which appears here. All are from Harrington's line of "theatrical" figurals and show the influence of modern dance and dramatic movement on her work. Particularly notable is the exquisite attention to detail that distinguishes a Ceramic Arts Studio piece. Betty Harrington not only created the CAS designs, but also did the actual mold work. She was thus able to make certain that even the most minute aspects of a design—such as "Zor" and "Zorina's" realistic fabric draping or the wave-like folds of "Water Man's" robe— were carried through from start to finish. Ceramic Art Studio theatrical figures are larger than life, and need just the right stage settings to convey their sense of high drama. Providing those settings are the equally theatrical—and equally stunning—Moss lamps.

It'll Cost You!

While a Decoramic figurine isn't going to add much to the asking price of a Moss lamp (after all, most of these lamps are *supposed* to be figural), the more impressive the designer name, the more you can expect to pay. While the competition can be rough (what with lamp, '50s, and figurine collectors all in the running), some general **figurine-only** prices can help provide you with an idea of the current market. (And, should you find a figure *plus* a lamp at these prices, don't hesitate—grab it!)

Hedi Schoop's "Phantasy" ladies currently average over $300 per pair, with "Poodle Girl" fetching $150-175. The deLee Art "Siamese Dancers" are also in the $300-per-pair range, with Lefton and Yona figures more affordably priced at $75-100 each. Ceramic Arts Studio figurines can be conservatively priced at $150-200 for the "Zor" and "Zorina" duo, $200 for "Water Man", and (are you ready for this) at least $600 for "Adonis and Aphrodite"! (Remember, that's not including the lamps.) However, for the determined cross-collector, the little bit extra (!) for a figure you've fallen in love with is always worth it!

. . . and by the way, should you run across Moss aquarium coffee table #6, with Dorothy Kindell's "Sahara Girl" waiting patiently for the flood and the fish, just keep it to yourself, OK? And give me a call!

Original inventory photo of the "Oriental Girl and Boy" figurines by Decoramic Kilns, #208 F, #208 M. Used with great regularity, these figurines show up on a wide variety of Moss lamps.

Detail, "Oriental Girl".

Detail, "Oriental Boy".

#X 212 F "Mambo" by Decoramic Kilns, on lamp #SR 74.

"Mambo" in color, on lamp #XT 801. 2' 10" h. *Photo by Heather Jeche. Courtesy of Richard A. Elioff*

Detail, "Mambo".

The "Cocktail Girl" goes solo on floor lamp #2317. 5' 1" h. *Courtesy of Jeff Bukas*

Decoramic's "Cocktail Girl", #205 F, with "Escort" #205 M.

The "Escort" gets a night off. #T 579 M. 4' 2" h. *Courtesy of Meshell Jesse, 20/60 Modern*

Left: He also gets around! Decoramic's "Escort" makes time with another companion, dubbed "Marilyn" by collectors. #206 F, #206 M.

Right: "Marilyn" strikes a demure pose on lamp # T 632.

Let's dance! Decoramic "Ballet Pair", #201 F, #201 M.

Private dancer? "Ballet Man" on lamp #XT 802. 3' 4" h. *Photo courtesy of William J. Burke*

Same pair, different costumes. #207 F, #207 M.

Here he is—once more in the spotlight—"Ballet Man" on floor lamp #2316.

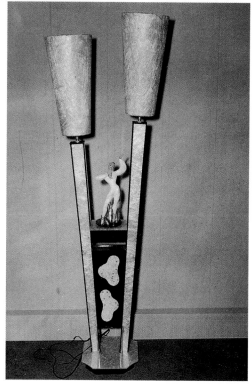

They ring their chimes on many lamps: the Decoramic "Bell Girl" #202 F, and "Bell Boy" #202 M.

"Bell Girl" on lamp #XT 803.

Detail, "Bell Boy". *Photo by Cheryl M. Gorski. Courtesy of Brenda Jackson Boyd*

The "Bell Boy" in blue, on lamp #T 543. 2' 10-1/2" h. *Photo courtesy of William J. Burke*

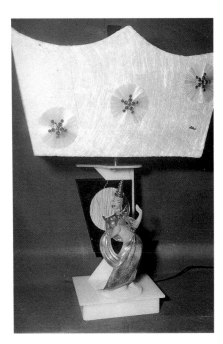

Decoramic "Temple Dancers", #203 M, #203 F.

Female "Temple Dancer" struts her stuff on lamp #SR 73.

"Temple Dancer" in white and gold, on pink plexi. #XT 855, with music box. 2' 7" h. *Courtesy of Jeff Bukas*

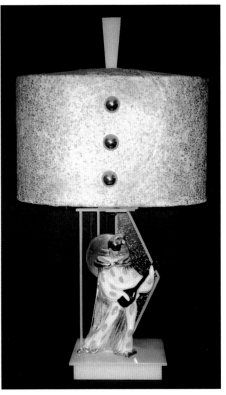

Early Elvis? Decoramic "Minstrels", #200 F, #200 M.

The masked musician in concert! Male "Minstrel" on lamp #XT 804. 2' 9" h. *Photo courtesy of William J. Burke*

Decoramic "Prom Girl", #X 211 F, on lamp #T 731. 3' 7-1/2" h. *Courtesy of Jeff Bukas*

Decoramic "Rhumba Dancers", #209 M, #209 F.

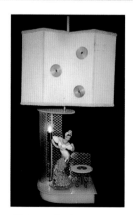

Boom-chicka-boom! Female "Rhumba Dancer", lamp #T 617. 2' 10" h. *Photo courtesy of William J. Burke*

"Thai Dancers" by Decoramic Kilns, #204 M, #204 F.

"Dervish Couple" by Decoramic, #210 M, #210 F.

The Yona—that is, DECORAMIC—version of the "Bali Dancer", on #T 681. 3' 4" h. *Courtesy of Joe Anthony and Marie Christine Londrico*

On the inventory photo for Moss smoking stand #4635, this figure is identified as #319 "Bali Dancer" by Yona.

The "Bali Dancer" is also clearly marked "Yona" on table lamp #XT 810. (The unique horizontal shades on this lamp can be adjusted to suit your lighting preference.) 1' 2" h. x 3' 1" w. *Courtesy of Jeff Bukas*

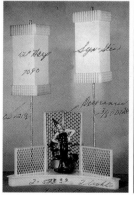

By the time lamp #T 681 hit the market, it had become more economical to use less expensive figurines, similar (!) to those by "name" designers. In other words, this may look like Yona's "Bali Dancer", but it isn't. It's a close relation, produced by Decoramic Kilns.

Also by Yona: "Girl with Basket", lamp #XT 811. 2' h. *Photo courtesy of William J. Burke*

35

Lefton "Asian Dancer" on lamp #XT 805. 2' 5" h. *Photo courtesy of Amy Paliwoda*

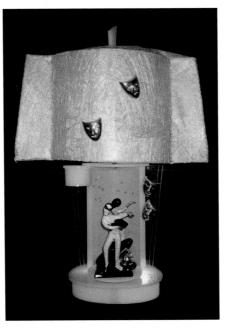

Lefton "Harlequinade Boy", #1379, a popular figure on many Moss lamps, shown here on music box lamp #T 534. (The melody played? "The Continental"!) 2' 5" h. *Photo courtesy of William J. Burke*

"Harlequinade Girl", #1379, also on #T 534. Both figures appear on this music box lamp, with the revolve determining who faces out. *Photo courtesy of William J. Burke*

Ad from the February, 1956 issue of *The Gift and Art Buyer*. "Harlequinade" pair #1379 is shown at top right.

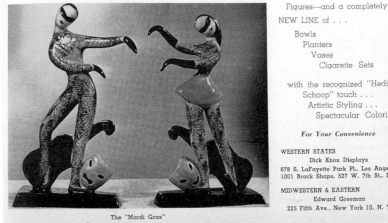

Great minds think alike? This Hedi Schoop "Mardi Gras" pair predates the Lefton duo. The advertisement is from the June, 1951 issue of *The Gift and Art Buyer*.

Moss wall plaque #5001 with Hedi Schoop "Dancer", #319/20.

A much-desired Moss Lamp figurine: Hedi Schoop's "Poodle Girl" on #XT 806. 2' 7-1/2" h. *Photo courtesy of William J. Burke*

The Moss planter is #5000. The figure is Hedi Schoop's "Lotus Lee Fan Girl", #228/9.

Opposite page: The ethereal "Phantasy Lady" by Hedi Schoop, on Moss Lamp #XT 807. 2' 5-1/2" h. *Courtesy of Joe Anthony and Marie Christine Londrico*

Hedi Schoop "Lantern Man" lights up Moss lamp #XT 808. 2' 8" h. *Courtesy of Jeff Bukas*

The "Musician" from Hedi Schoop's "Young China" pair. The figurines date from the 1940s. #XT 813. 2' 7" h. *Piña collection*

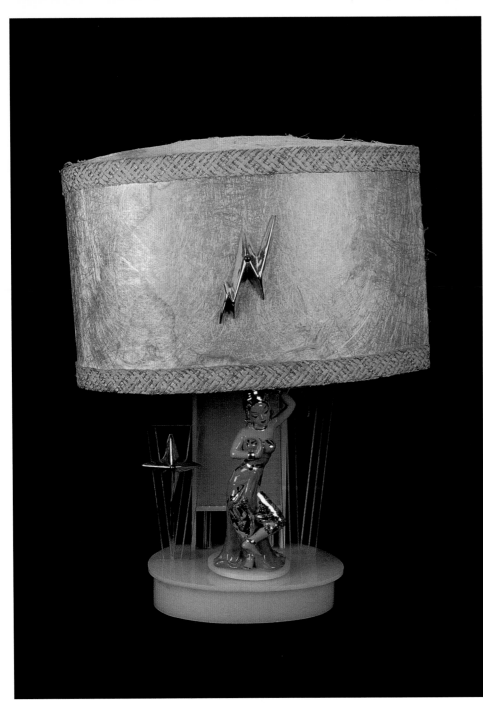

The female half of the "Siamese Dancers" by deLee Art strikes an uncomfortable pose on lamp #T 476. 2' 6" h. *Courtesy of Joe Anthony and Marie Christine Londrico*

Hot, hot, hot! The Ceramic Arts Studio "Fire Woman" adorns table lamp #XT 859. 1' 7 1/2" h. *Courtesy of Jeff Bukas.*

At least her partner gets to keep both feet on the ground. The deLee "Siamese Dancers".

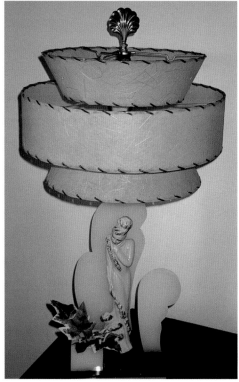

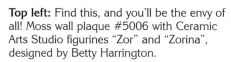

Top left: Find this, and you'll be the envy of all! Moss wall plaque #5006 with Ceramic Arts Studio figurines "Zor" and "Zorina", designed by Betty Harrington.

Bottom left: Catch the wave! Ceramic Arts Studio "Water Man", a stationary figurine on lamp #XT 809. 2' 4" h. *Johnson collection*

Top right: The exquisite "Adonis and Aphrodite", designed by Betty Harrington for Ceramic Arts Studio. Estimated value: $600/pr. *Johnson collection*

Bottom right: "Adonis and Aphrodite", posed gracefully on #XT 856. 2' 7" h.

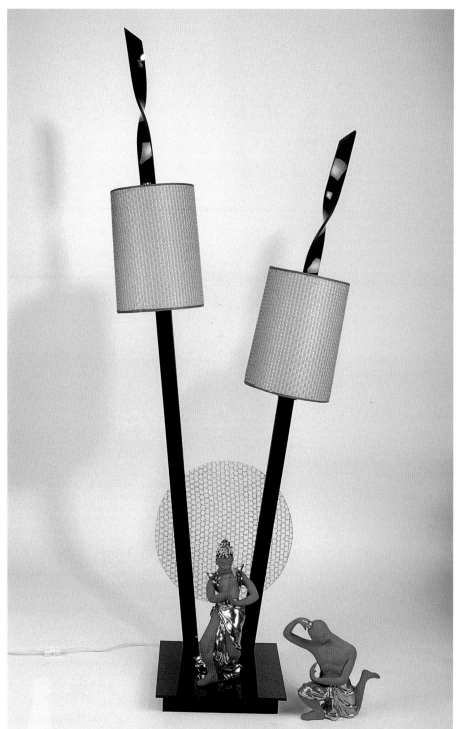

A combination of glazed and unglazed finishes, identified as by "The Bennetts, Caroline & Bud, CA". #XT 812. 4' 2" h. *Courtesy of Jeff Bukas*

Top right: Hope she's holding her breath! Dorothy Kindell's "Sahara Girl", #80, submerged in Moss aquarium table #6.

Center right: Another juxtaposition of glazed and unglazed finishes sets off this "Native Man" by Consolidated, #759. The Moss plaque is #5007.

Bottom right: Ever wonder where butterfly fish come from? These come from Ceramic Craft, #191, and adorn Moss room divider #3501.

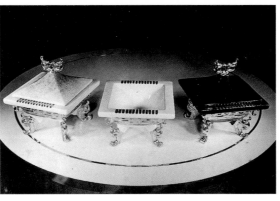

Ashtrays intended for coffee table use, designed for Moss by "Lyn of California Ceramics". Two #4020 ashtrays bracket #4019.

An early supplier of ceramic ashtrays for Moss smokestands was Marvin Charles. These are ready and waiting on stand #4633.

#4019 by Lyn

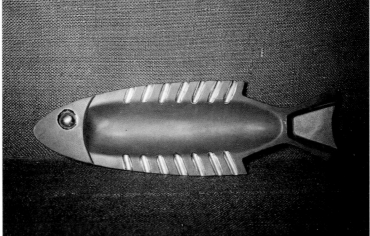

#4013

Also by Lyn, #3006

#3002

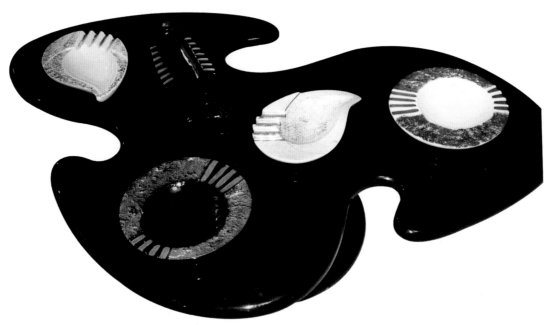

In living color: #4013, #3006, #3002.

CHAPTER 4

"POSITIVELY ELECTRIC:
OTHER MOSS FEATURES & PRODUCTS"

We used to say you could probably do better having a repair shop to take care of all that Moss stuff than you could selling lamps!

Sid Bass,
former sales representative,
Rembrandt Lamps

Moss lamps lit up. They came with statues. And they spun around. . . but was that really enough? Thelma and Gerry Moss, and the talented Moss designers and craftsmen, were always searching out new ideas and new ways of capturing and maintaining the public's interest in Moss products. This meant expanding the basic Moss menu beyond plexiglas table and floor lamps, into previously uncharted territory.

Some of the new ideas, such as floor-to-ceiling ("pole") lamps and hanging lamps, were adaptations of concepts already standard in the lighting industry. Even here, however, the ideas were given an unexpected Moss twist: there are pole lamps, and then there is Moss pole lamp #2378, with a birdcage-encased "Marilyn" trapped midway between floor and ceiling. But that was only the beginning . . .

In with the Old

A Moss spin on the traditional occurred in the early 1960s, with the introduction of the ceramic-based "Tami" lamps. This re-embrace of the past was prompted by a slump in plexiglas lamp sales, the result of a backlash in consumer taste. For many young moderns of the Camelot years, plexiglas lamps smacked too heavily of the decor at Mom and Dad's; Tami lamps were seen as a step forward. They came in a variety of pleasant finishes (mirror, smoked, and clear), blended well with almost every decorating scheme, and, even at $79.95 retail, were considered money well spent.

Today the urn-like Tamis, topped with sober cylindrical shades, seem much less forward-looking than their plexiglas predecessors. However, they are favorites with those who collect 1960s decor paraphernalia, and the much-subdued Tami styling still remains identifiably Moss. Check out the oriental motif on Tami #55 A, or the clever use of curved line on #52 A; it's possible to

see the same design influences at work here that also resulted in the better-known Moss plexiglas lamps.

Don't 'Leaf' Home without One!

The leaf lamps started out for Sears, but after awhile we shipped them all over.

Jerry Slater

Another traditional look ("traditional" in the Moss sense of the word) can be seen in the company's "leaf lamps" of the late '40s and early '50s. While plexiglas, the leaf lamps are simpler in design than the rest of the Moss line and were initially designed expressly to catch the interest of Sears Roebuck & Co. catalog customers. It was assumed that the typical Sears customer might like to spruce up the home place with a modern touch—as long as it wasn't *too* modern. The leaf lamps, with their gently curving calla lily-like leaves of plexi, filled the bill. No whirling figurines or dustings of glitter here. The leaf lamp could be successfully transplanted into almost any home, without making the rest of the decor look hopelessly out of date.

Not surprisingly, what was intended for one consumer base found popularity with others as well. Leaf lamps not only sold successfully to Sears buyers, but also became part of the mainstream Moss line; floor, table, pole, and smokestand versions were produced. The reason lies in their classic simplicity: the central lamp stem on #2250, for instance, seems a natural outgrowth of the white plexi leaves surrounding it. This innate unity of concept and execution struck a common chord with buyers across catalog lines.

Music, Music, Music!

Even among the tone-deaf, one of the most sought-after of Moss lamps is the "music box lamp", which did everything a regular Moss lamp did, and more! Billed as "another Moss innovation", each of these table lamps was equipped with a "Golden Tone Music Box". By pulling on a brass ball, lamp owners could enjoy the tinkling strains of popular standards as the figurines whirled. Most of the music boxes continue to function today, and, in some cases, it's possible to pinpoint the year the lamp was introduced by the tune it played. The first version of #T 534 shown in this chapter plays "Heart", from the musical *Damn Yankees*. As the show premiered on Broadway in 1955, this lamp evidently joined the Moss chorus line sometime after that.

All the Bells & Whistles

In their quest to explore every possible way a Moss lamp could be a Moss lamp "and then some", the Moss designers experimented with some intriguing possibilities. There were of course different lighting options: fluorescents in the stem; light-up bases and platforms; globes and starlite bulbs operating independently of the main light source; even lights on which the spun glass shades could be rotated, to cast interesting shadows on walls, ceilings, or party guests.

Then there were the lamps with special mechanical functions: the "Intercom Lamp", #T 627; lamps with double shades that revolve in opposite directions such as #T 689, or with revolving inner cores such as #3502; lamps with "spinner paddles" (#XT 850); TV lamps (#XT 851); and even radio lamps! A construction invoice for radio lamp #T 523 (similar to #XT 852 shown in this chapter) places the cost for parts and labor at $31.87, shade construction and assembly at $3.90. The selling price was $59.75 for the lamp, $10.75 for the shade. A nice profit then, a bargain today!

Tick, Tick. Splish, Splash. Glug, Glug.

Have to turn on the light to check the clock? How much handier if the clock is right there as part of the lamp! That's the theory behind the Moss clock lamps, a significant part of the company's output. Nearly 50 models are shown in the inventory section of *Moss Lamps* , ranging from wall, floor, and table models, to grandfather clocks, a "clock coffee table", and a "clock room divider"! Among the companies supplying the clockworks for Moss were Packard Bell, Lanshire, L. Harris, and Urgas.

Among the most coveted of Moss lamps, easily cascading into the $1000-$1500 price range, are the "waterworks". This category encompasses such novelties as fountains,

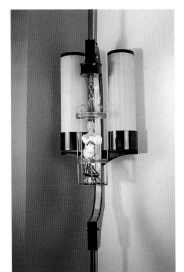

"Just a bird in a gilded cage". The unusual design of floor-to-ceiling pole lamp #2378 keeps "Marilyn" safe from her admirers. Full extension, 9'.
Courtesy of Jeff Bukas

waterwheels, and even aquariums—all included as part of an operating Moss lamp. The waterworks had their inspiration in a champagne fountain designed for the 1956 wedding of Carol Moss and Stan Goodstein. It attracted such favorable attention that variations were soon available for purchase. Of course, owning a Moss waterwork was not without its hazards. One customer of the mid-'50s purchased aquarium table #1, and removed the black plexiglas bars separating the table top from the fish tank for a "better fit". The next day, the irate owner reported that the aquarium table had "killed all her fish". (Evidently, the fact that they might need air hadn't occurred to her!) The "fish-killer" sold at retail for $379.

Most awesome of all were the Moss "bar lamps", and leading the list in impressiveness was #6001, the "Fish Tank Bar". Not just a bar, not just a fish tank, not just a lamp, the "Fish Tank Bar" was a combination of all three! This watery wonder took 10 hours and 45 minutes to assemble (labor cost, $35.20), used $57 worth of material, and from the looks of it was worth every penny—plus plenty more. The original sales price of the "Fish Tank Bar" was $199.75, less than one-tenth of its current market value. The bar lamps were labor-intensive to make (even the non-fish tank #6000 took 12-1/2 hours to construct), and are in short supply today. If you find one, congratulations! Buy yourself a drink.

These Also Served

Had enough? Wait, there's more! Moss coffee and end tables. Moss wall plaques and planters . . . Moss room dividers . . . Moss plexiglas lighters. Each made its own distinct contribution to the Moss line, and each offers an excellent example of the wonders that can happen when imagination, electrical expertise—and plexiglas—combine!

In the post-modern era of the 1950s, the idea was that function need not be threatened by a more adventurous expression of form. Abstract expressionist design did not necessarily displace function.

Sheila Steinberg & Kate Dooner
Fabulous Fifties: Designs for Modern Living

Function? Form? Abstract expressionist design? With a Moss multipurpose lamp, you could have them all—and all at once!

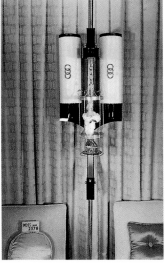

Inventory photo of #2378.

Traditional looks begin here: original Tami lamp mold from the Moss studio.

Three versions of Tami # 77 A. Available color combinations were described as "two-tone blue drip glaze, two-tone brown drip glaze, and two-tone blue-grey to amethyst" each with "matching iridescent sub-base". 4' 3" h.

Tami lamp #55 A, depicting an oriental scene. 3' 10" h.

#55 A in brown lustre.

Tami lamp #74 A, available in iridescent blue, lavender, or rust, with gold or silver leaf bases. Original selling price, $23.75. Each, 3' 5" h.

#85 A and #86 A offer unusual ceramic texturing. Each, 3' 7" h.

46

Left: From the Moss home: Tami #52 A.

Right: Original inventory photo, #52 A.

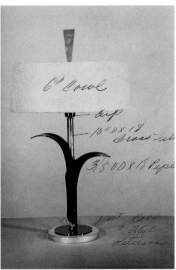

Inventory photo of #T 688, in black plexi.

A staple of the Sears catalogs in the late 1940s: the Moss "Leaf Lamp", shown here in its table version, #T 688. 2' 3" h. *Courtesy of Jeff Bukas*

47

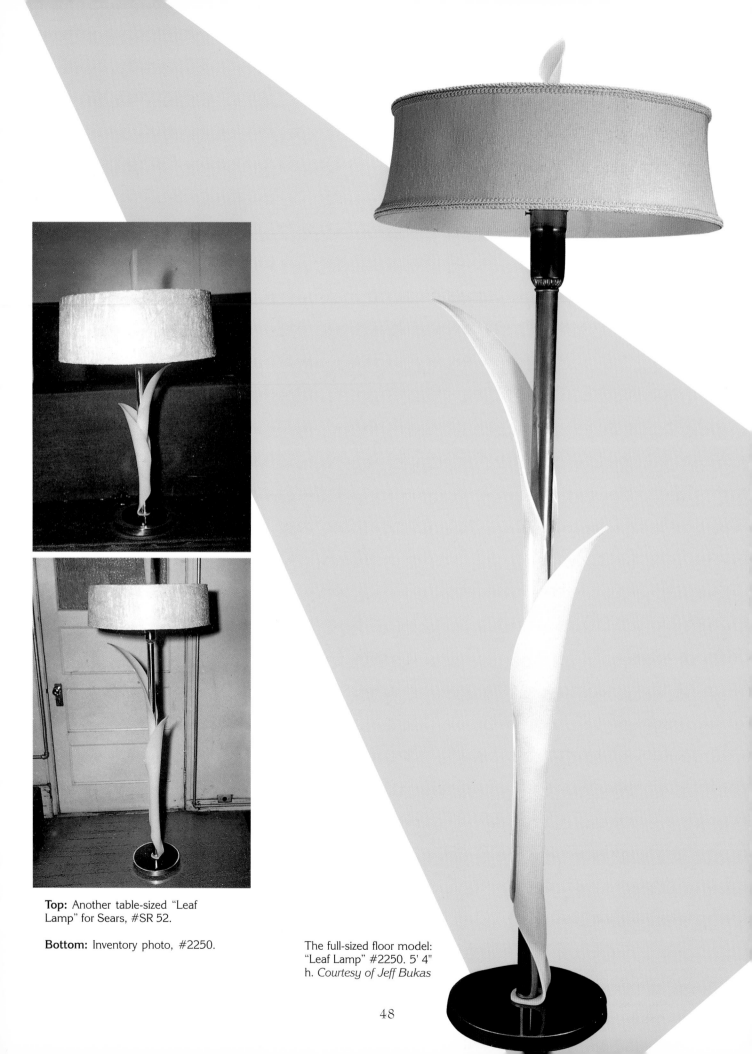

Top: Another table-sized "Leaf Lamp" for Sears, #SR 52.

Bottom: Inventory photo, #2250.

The full-sized floor model: "Leaf Lamp" #2250. 5' 4" h. *Courtesy of Jeff Bukas*

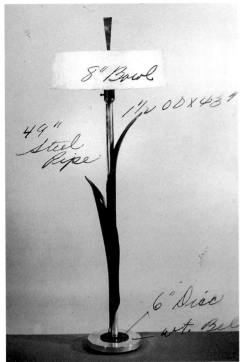

The black plexi floor model, #2363. 4' 11-1/2" h.

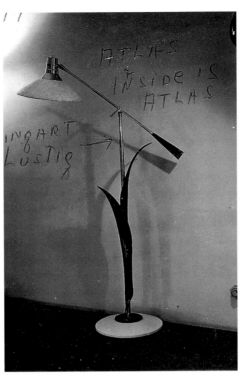

#2277, a "Leaf Lamp" with adjustable shade arm.

Floor-to-ceiling "Leaf Lamp" with hanging birdcage lanterns, #2326. This one also appears in the 1961 Moss catalog.

#2326 in color. Full extension, 9'. *Courtesy of Joe Anthony and Marie Christine Londrico*

For Sears smokers, a "Leaf Lamp" smoking stand. The ashtrays are by Marvin Charles. #4629.

49

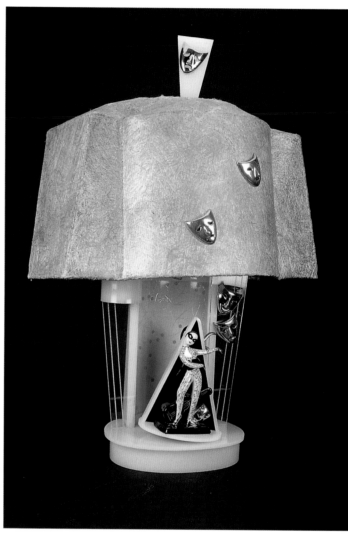

#XT 848, a pink and black plexi table lamp, equipped with "Golden Tone Music Box". The song played, probably "Cocktail Girl's" favorite, is "Si, Si". 2' 9" h. *Courtesy of Jeff Bukas*

A frequently seen music box lamp, #T 534, featured in the 1961 catalog. This one plays "Heart". Here, Lefton's "Harlequinade Boy" is facing out. 2' 5" h. *Courtesy of Joe Anthony and Marie Christine Londrico*

. . . and now it's "Harlequinade Girl's" turn.

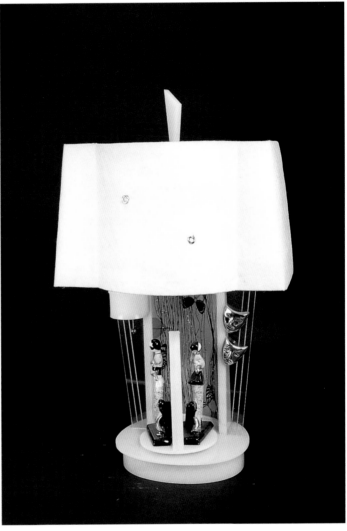

"The music goes 'round and 'round'". Caught in mid-turn are both of #T 534's "Harlequinade" figures. (By the way, the tune on **this** "Golden Tone" is "Tico Tico".) *Courtesy of Jeff Bukas*

Here's Hedi Schoop's "Dancer" on music box table lamp #XT 849. The hit parade selection is "Stardust". 2' 7" h. *Photo courtesy of William J. Burke*

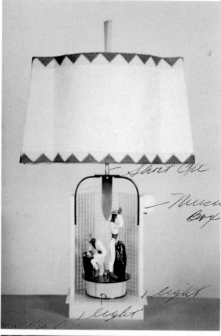

Inventory photo of music box lamp #T 684 with calypso figurines. There's no mention of the melody played, but something with a tropical beat is probably a safe bet! 2' 10-1/2" h.

Yona's "Bali Dancer" on music box lamp #T 667. 2' 7-1/2" h.

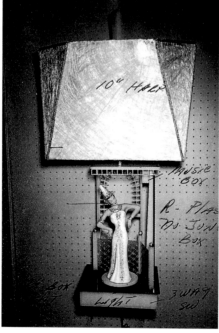

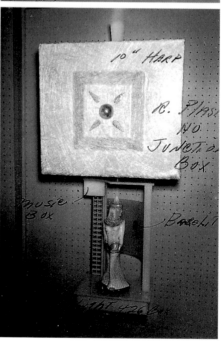

The Egyptian lady shuffles off to Babylon, to the strains of music box lamp #T 666. 2' 10" h.

"Cocktail Girl" hears your innermost thoughts in this unique lamp, which incorporates an **intercom** into its design. (It's assumed that purchase by the pair was required!) #T 627.

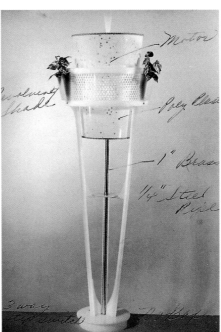

And one more revolving shade, this on floor model #2364.

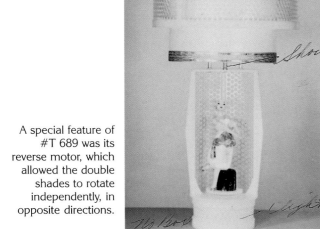

A special feature of #T 689 was its reverse motor, which allowed the double shades to rotate independently, in opposite directions.

Hanging lamps sometimes also offered hidden extras. While #3500, *left*, simply lights up, #3501, *center*, features revolving leaves. On #3502, *right*, the inner cone revolves.

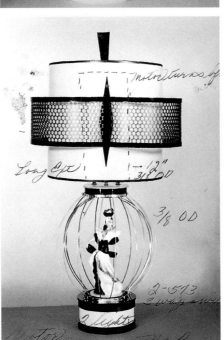

Another double shade with reverse motor, another lady in a cage. #T 686.

53

Adding interest to #XT 850 is the plexi spinner with "Comedy" and "Tragedy" faces, left of the masked ballerina. 2' 8" h. *Courtesy of Joe Anthony and Marie Christine Londrico*

A seldom-seen Moss TV lamp, complete with snarling panther, was spotted in the Moss' San Francisco home. The companion figurines were added by Mrs. Moss. #XT 851.

Hedi Schoop's "Poodle Girl" is back, this time adding her attractive presence to a Moss radio lamp, #XT 852. 2' 10" h. *Courtesy of Jeff Bukas*

#XT 815 clock lamp with deLee Art's "Siamese Dancer". 2' 11" h.

Bottom left: Spun glass forms the base of this Moss wall clock, #X 3102. 17" d. *Courtesy of Jeff Bukas*

Bottom center: Moss triangular table clock lamp with side planters, #3006. *Courtesy of Jeff Bukas*

Bottom right: Original inventory photo of #3006.

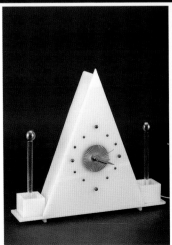

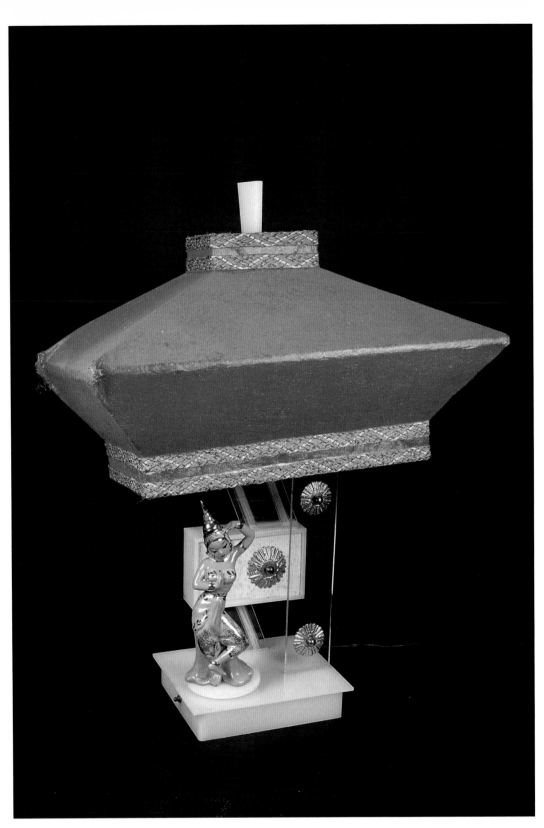

#XT 815, alternate shade. With clock lamp pairs, only one partner had a clock; for the other, a decorative panel was substituted. Here, the female "Siamese Dancer" goes clockless. *#XT 815 photos courtesy of Joe Anthony and Marie Christine Londrico*

A basic table clock model, #X 3101. 2' 9" h. *Photo courtesy of William J. Burke*

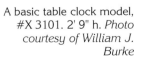

The inspiration for the Moss fountains: a champagne fountain designed especially for the 1956 wedding of Carol Moss and Stan Goodstein. *Courtesy of Carol and Stan Goodstein*

Terry inspects! Here, the Moss mascot checks out fountain lamp #T 699.

#XT 853 fountain in operation.

"Bali Dancer" gets ready to take the plunge on this elaborate fountain lamp, #XT 853. 4' 4" h.

Detail, #XT 853 "Bali Dancer", surrounded by starlite bulbs.

The shade of #XT 853, which combines spun glass with fabric insert panels. *#XT 853 photos by Cheryl M. Gorski. Courtesy of Brenda Jackson Boyd*

57

Moss aquarium lamp, complete with lionhead goldfish. A red light in the base gives the watery interior an eerie glow #XT 858. 2' 3" h. *Courtesy of Jeff Bukas*

Bottom left: Pastoral pleasures abound, with the Moss waterwheel lamp, #T 726. The base lights up as the wheel turns. 4' 2" h. *Courtesy of Jeff Bukas*

Bottom center: Inventory photo of #T 726. It's not clear if the additional figure at left came with the lamp, or was just paying a visit for the purposes of this photo.

Bottom right: The "fish killer": aquarium table #1.

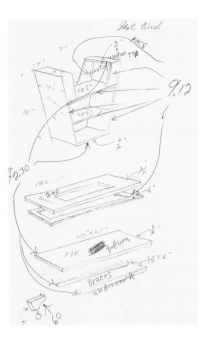

Drink like a fish? You'll love the Moss "Fish Tank Bar", #6001!

Original design sketch for the "Fish Tank Bar".

"Bar #6000" also allowed for plenty of liquid refreshment (but without the fish.)

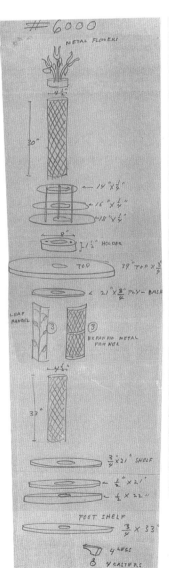

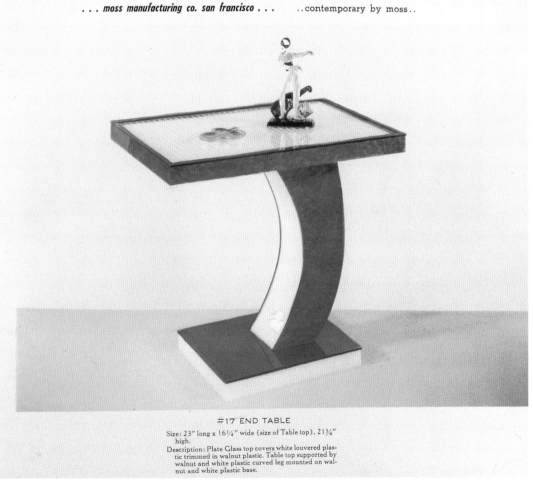

#17 END TABLE

Size: 23" long x 16¼" wide (size of Table top), 21¾" high.
Description: Plate Glass top covers white louvered plastic trimmed in walnut plastic. Table top supported by walnut and white plastic curved leg mounted on walnut and white plastic base.

This original design drawing for "Bar #6000", found in the Moss studio, was sketched on a brown paper bag!

One of the most attractive Moss end tables, #17, shown in this promotional photo from the 1950s. 1' 9-3/4" h.

Wall plaque planter #5002, with Hedi Schoop "Dancer". 2' 11" w. *Courtesy of Jeff Bukas*

Inventory photo, #5002.

An impressive Moss room divider, #2272, with spun glass "gong". 5' 4" h. x 2' 6" w. *Courtesy of Jeff Bukas*

#2272 inventory photo.

One-of-a-kind room divider with butterfly plexi panel, designed for the Moss home.

Two Moss plexiglas lighters are shown in this grouping, including one, *center left*, in a novel "piano" shape.

60

CHAPTER 5

"ENLIGHTENING INFO:
IDENTIFYING, LOCATING, & PRICING MOSS LAMPS"

"Is it Moss?" "Is it expensive?" "Is it available where I live?" These urgent inquiries (and more) are answered in:

The Moss Question Box!

QUESTION: I have a plexiglas lamp with no identifying markings at all. How do I know if it's Moss?
ANSWER: You don't, but you can make a good guess. Not every Moss lamp has a "Moss Mfg." stamp on the base interior. If you want to take the motor housing apart, chances are good there'll be a Moss imprint on the motor. And, if the lamp was made for sale in California, the junction box was required to carry the Moss I.D. However, in the absence of the above, or any such dead giveaways as inventory tags, use your own best judgment. If the body is plexi, the shade spun glass, and there's a ceramic figurine, chances are good it's Moss.

QUESTION: I want to collect everything Moss ever made. What are my chances?
ANSWER: That depends on your life expectancy. If it's Yoda-like, you may be successful. If it's the same as everybody else's, you'll take what you can get and like it. According to former Moss employees, there were probably *1000* different Moss models released over the years, with new additions to the line semiannually. These are the plexiglass products; not included are the 100 or so Tami lamps, the "traditional" Moss lamps issued in the late 30s and early 40s, and such *tchotchkes* as ceramic ashtrays and plexi lighters. Additionally, a number of the Moss models were "one-of-a-kind", samples put together for display to furniture dealers checking out the Moss line at the major market shows. If no orders were placed, the sample was sold, and no more were made. So with certain Moss lamps, you could possibly end up with "the one and only"!

QUESTION: 1000 models, huh? Are they all shown in this book?
ANSWER: Are you crazy? Actually, a significant number are represented here, not only in new photos from collections around the country, but also in the original inventory shots that comprise Part II. These vintage black-and-white photos, many of which carry original assembly notes, are from employee reference notebooks. Although a factory

operation, Moss Manufacturing relied on individual fabrication, rather than automated production. Thus, inventory photos were necessary to make sure the quality and design of each lamp was consistent.

The inventory books from which *Moss Lamps* drew its photos were located by accident, behind a paint booth in the Moss workroom. It's presumed that more books, depicting the remainder of the inventory, originally existed, but were discarded over the years.

QUESTION: So without the books, how did you come up with all the inventory numbers?
ANSWER: For the purposes of easy reference, it was determined that all lamps shown in *Moss Lamps* needed an inventory number. It's much simpler to refer to a #2310 than to "that floor lamp where the back angles, and it's white, and it's black, and there's this man with his hands folded, and he spins. And it lights up." Many of the assembly photos gave the original inventory number. The most significant numerical designations are:

T: precedes all table lamp numbers
A: follows all Tami lamp numbers
SR: precedes the number on lamps designed specifically for Sears
1-100: occasional tables
2000 SERIES: floor and floor-to-ceiling lamps, room dividers
3000 SERIES: clocks
3500 SERIES: hanging lamps
4000 SERIES: smokestands
5000 SERIES: wall plaques
6000 SERIES: bars

Naturally, there's some overlap: a table lamp may have a clock, but still be a table lamp with a "T" designation. And for some reason, the "Lyn of California" ceramic ashtrays were also originally given "3000" number assignments . . . but it's usually easy enough to tell an ashtray from a clock!

For objects that did not appear in the 1961 catalog or in the reference photos, numbers in the proper category have been newly assigned; these begin well above the highest known original inventory numbers. Newly-assigned reference numbers are each preceded by an "X". (Should the missing original numbers some day be luckily discovered, you can plug those in and "X" their predecessors out!)

QUESTION: So do the lamps all appear in numerical order?
ANSWER: Now that wouldn't be very appealing, would it? Organization in *Moss Lamps* is by style. Since shades and figurines were often interchangeable, the categorizations that proved most practical and consistent were by base or stem. In both the color and black-and-white table lamp inventory sections of this book, grouping is by base shape (square, round, stepped, irregular-shaped, and so on). Multi-shaded, non-figural, and lantern lamps are also clustered together. For floor lamps, the division is simpler: angled stem, straight stem, metal base, lanterns, and multi-shaded.

In other categories, the arrangements follow common sense: wall clocks together, Tami lamps with identical body shapes together, and the like. The goal has been to provide a reference guide both easy to use, and adaptable to the addition of future Moss lamp discoveries.

QUESTION: Did anybody else make lamps like these?
ANSWER: Just like? Not so far as we know. Sort of like? Well, there was always somebody willing to give it a try:

There were other lines that used plexi—Modeline, and there was one out of St. Louis, another out of Kentucky that I know of. There was also a guy down the hall from us the in the Merchandise Mart, and he carried a lot of that stuff, but it was very low-end. Not like Moss. They never went in for low-end.

Sid Bass

There was one company in southern California—Milo—and they tried to knock us off. Of course, Milo knocked off everybody. "Inspired" by Moss. That's putting it nicely.

Carol Moss Goodstein

An example of another company's plaster-and-metal spinning lamp is shown in this chapter, as is an unaccredited magazine rack incorporating a spun glass moon. Fortunately, however, the Moss style (and quality) are quite distinctive.

Also included here are several samples of imaginative '50s lamps by Moss contemporaries working in other media, such as the plaster lamps of Continental Arts. Are they attractive? Certainly. Are they worth collecting? Most definitely. Are they Moss? Are you kidding?

QUESTION: So where can I find Moss lamps?
ANSWER: Often, where you least expect: at an Omaha garage sale—a Soho street fair—your neighbor's house. An antiques dealer in Glendale, California, noted that she found seven Moss lamps in one home—the only trace of the *outré* in an otherwise staidly decorated environment. As Moss lamps were offered for sale at each year's major furniture markets in such cities as San Francisco, New York, Chicago, Los Angeles, and Dallas, metro areas are also a good bet. And, in the non-acquisitive sense, it's fun "finding" Moss lamps when they pop up as part of the decor in fictional settings. Moss lamps have played supporting roles in such movies as *From Here To Eternity; To Wong Foo, Thanks For Everything, Julie Newmar;* and *Blue in the Face.* One glimpse of a Moss lamp in the background can provide a world of insight into a movie character's character!

QUESTION: One last thing: I suppose these lamps cost a lot?
ANSWER: Well, yes, if the seller knows what he has, and it's in good or repairable condition; no, if you find your lamp at a house sale, or it's in need of considerable restoration. I was once offered a Moss lamp with a Ceramic Arts figure missing its legs, for $600. That's not the same as being offered the same lamp and figure with all limbs present and accounted for. The prices given in the *Moss Lamps* Index are intended only as a starting point at which to begin negotiations. They represent an average of actual selling prices, with factors such as rarity, additional functions, and figurines entering into the estimates given. You may encounter prices that are higher than these. Hopefully, you'll run across at least a few that are lower!

In a Fall, 1995 *Echoes* magazine profile, Sheila Steinberg, co-author of *Fabulous Fifties: Designs for Modern Living* noted that as recently as 1988 she was able to affordably accent her '50s-themed Manhattan apartment with copious numbers of Moss lamps found at street fairs, flea markets, and prop houses. Today, however, even the seediest spots are wising up. You may yet find that "Fish Tank Bar" for under $100 . . . but don't hold your breath.

Oops—the Moss Question Box is all full. We'll have to empty it, and get back to you later!

The same logo, here stamped on a separate piece affixed to a black plexiglas base.

Moss imprint, stamped on interior of plexiglas base. The inscription reads "Protected by United States and Canadian patents. Copyrighted Moss Mfg. Co, San Francisco, Calif." Many Moss lamps carry this identifying mark (except those that don't!).

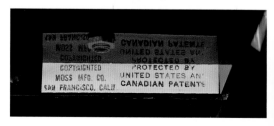

An original Moss Lamps tag and keychain. The keychain bears the original "1124 Mission Street" address.

Reverse of tag and keychain. Sales and model information was entered on each tag.

Early sales tags from the "house of lamps and light".

Top: Moss sales representative's card. Mentioned are the company's showrooms in "San Francisco, New York, Chicago, Toronto, Los Angeles, and Boston". *Bottom:* plastic Moss Lamps tag; music box tag. Music box lamp owners were informed "This lamp equipped with a golden tone music box. PULL BRASS BALL DOWN AND RELEASE. Another Moss innovation."

What the competition was doing: Continental Arts ballerina lamp. 2' 10" h.

Sometimes other companies also experimented with the revolving lamp idea. The unidentified manufacturer of this 1950s lamp utilizes a revolving pair similar to those on Moss #T 534. However, the base is chalk, and the decorative attachments are all metal. The shade is fiberglass. 3' 2" h. *Photo courtesy of Denis Christiansen and Alan Trickett*

Detail, revolving figurine.

64

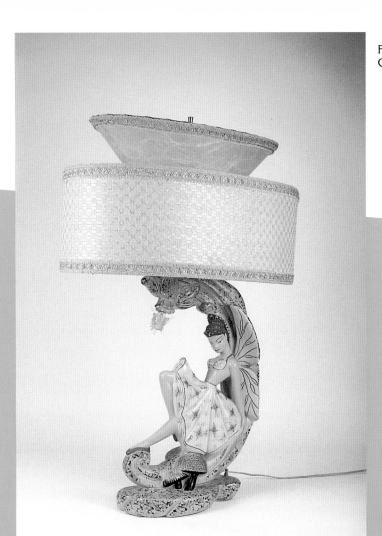

Fairy lamp, attributed to
Continental. 2' 8-1/2" h.

Continental Arts "Sunbathers".
2' 9-1/2" h.

Italian "lily" lamp. 2' 10" h.

Unidentified manufacturer, plaster figural lamp with carved wood-like texture. 2' 11" h.

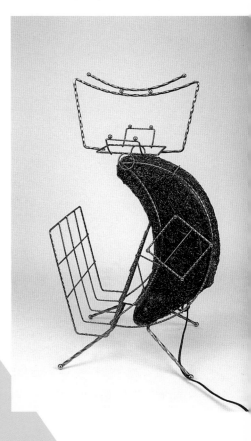

The wonders of spun glass! Another company has used their own version of this Moss mainstay, to create a crescent moon lamp/magazine rack. No home should be without one!
Period lamps courtesy of Joe Anthony and Marie Christine Londrico

"Panther" lamp, attributed to Moss. Although the panther looks familiar (see the TV lamp in Chapter 4), the wood base and shade do not. 2' h.

Who knows where you'll run across a Moss lamp? This pair, #XT 814, were on sale at a weekend antiques fair in New York's Chelsea district, November, 1998. Asking price? $250 for both.

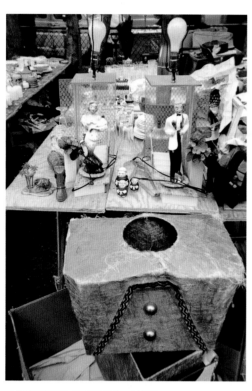

Available at California's Glendale Modernism Show in March of 1999 were the #T 579 pair. Each, 4' 2" h.

Also at Glendale, #T 543 M, 2' 6" h.

And his partner, #T 543 F. $495, and the pair could be yours! *Glendale Modernism Show photos courtesy of Meshell Jesse, 20/60 Modern*

The "Cocktail Girl", looking luscious on #X 2404, which features a unique use of pink plexiglas. This lamp was seen in the movie *Blue in the Face.* 5' 1" h. *Courtesy of Jeff Bukas*

Chapter 6

"Don't Pull the Plug!
Moss Lamp Reconditioning & Repair"

Jeff Bukas not only collects Moss lamps, he rejuvenates them. Over the years, the ravages of daily service have left many a Moss looking less than its best. Spun glass shades have become unspun. Plexiglas pieces have cracked or broken off. Motors no longer work. Some folks would bid such battered relics goodbye. Jeff Bukas gets them going again.

From his lamp-filled Chicago home, Bukas continues to perfect the art of the Moss makeover. Such resuscitation efforts not only increase the value of Moss lamps, but, more importantly, restore them to their rightful positions as brilliant design icons of an earlier age. For even the less than technically adept, Mr. Bukas' "rules for renovation" are concise, easy-to-follow, and ultimately rewarding. Here's what the restoration expert has to say about . . .

Those Hideously Hairy Shades

"When planning to repair a spun glass shade, first clean it well. If there is dust on the shade, a repair adhesive can darken it. Try using a can of compressed air to blow off the dust. You may also try light vacuuming with a brush attachment. (This also works well on fabric shades.) I sometimes use a clean, new paintbrush to sweep the dust off. Most importantly, BE CAREFUL! Do *not* try to wash a spun glass shade; it will fall apart in water.

Next, if possible, trim any small flyaway fibers. For fibers that are coming undone, apply water-based glue or acrylic gel medium. Shades with sunken tops can sometimes be strengthened with a mixture of one part water to one part glue (again, water-based). Work from the inside of the shade on a non-stick surface—I have used waxed paper or aluminum foil. If the shade has a flat top or flat surface, place that side down. Apply the glue mixture with a brush, and, of course, work on just one side at a time. (Collector William J. Burke also reports success with a hand-smoothed application of spray starch.) Allow the shade to dry thoroughly before picking it up or before proceeding with work on another area.

If a shade has been damaged beyond repair, but the metal frame is intact, a lamp shop can recover it with new or vintage fabric. This can be expensive, and there is no longer the authenticity of spun glass, but the visual appeal often makes it worthwhile. If a lamp is shadeless, suitable replacement shades of the period can usually be picked up inexpensively at antique stores and flea markets."

You'll Wonder Where the Yellow Went

"Over the years, cigarette smoke, dust, and grease particles have often left a yellowy buildup on the plexiglas portions of Moss lamps. This can usually be removed by applying a mixture of mild soap and water with a soft cloth. If the film proves stubborn, alternate wiping with a damp cloth, then a dry cloth, and keep repeating until the surface shines. You may also use commercial cleaners intended specifically for plastic and acrylic. Do *not* use any abrasives, as scratches are nearly impossible to disguise, especially on clear or black plexi. Also, do *not* use any cleaners that contain ammonia or alcohol. Although they may appear to clean well, the surface of plexiglas is actually (and permanently) damaged by these chemicals, resulting in eventual crazing and clouding. (Most glass cleaners contain ammonia or alcohol, and thus should not be used.) Once the decades of dirt have been removed, you can keep your Moss lamps dust-free with the regular use of a dampened cloth.

If a plexiglas piece is broken, the *only* means of repair is the application of an acrylic solvent cement. These special adhesives work differently than other glues: as the description indicates, they actually "dissolve" portions of the plexi, thus allowing bonding to occur. One product I've found that works particularly well is 'Craftics Acrylic Solvent Cement'. It's available at companies that sell acrylic and plexiglas products and requires a special applicator; you many want to ask the supplier for tips on how best to apply it!

If your lamp is missing a full or partial plexi segment, an acrylic or plexiglas supplier may be able to cut a replacement piece for you from a similar acrylic material. However, the new piece may appear a bit brighter than existing pieces already on the lamp. That's understandable: it just hasn't been around as long!"

Whirr . . . Whirr . . . Rattle, Rattle, Clank

"If a Moss lamp's 'spin motor' is noisy, non-working, or just non-existent, you may be out of luck. Until Moss Lighting closed its doors for good in 1998, it was sometimes possible to obtain replacement motors from existing inventory. Currently, my best suggestion is that you ask at a clock repair shop if similar motors are available. (Clock shops, incidentally, offer your best available option for getting the mechanics of a Moss lamp repaired.) Should the motor be operable, but the metal connector attaching the spin base to the lamp platform is missing or damaged, hardware store service technicians or friendly metalworkers can often be prevailed upon to rig up or construct replacement pieces. And, if a motor just whirrs instead of works, a last resort may be to disconnect its wiring and turn a non-spinning figure into a permanently stationary one."

Reconfigurations

"The figures on a Moss lamp have naturally been subjected to the same environmental influences as the plexiglas. Mild soap and water, applied with a soft cloth, can usually restore their luster. For easier cleaning, unbolt the figurines from their bases. Don't 'soak' the figures or wipe too vigorously, as many have features painted over the glaze. A thorough scrubbing could leave your figure faceless! Also, gold detailing often rubs off if cleaned too energetically, as will the finish of the gold ceramic stars, balls, bells, and so on, that accent many lamps and shades.

It's often possible to repair damaged figurines, depending on the extent of the damage, and assuming no pieces are missing. If the break is clean, glue the parts back together with an adhesive specifically intended for ceramic or china repair. If the figurine is an especially valuable one, you may wish to utilize the services of a professional. While ceramic repair experts can be pricey, a $600 Ceramic Arts "Adonis and Aphrodite" pair is probably well worth the investment!

Should the figure be missing significant body chunks, and thus be unrepairable, there's always a good chance of finding identical replacement figures, particularly if the original is by a 'name' such as Hedi Schoop or deLee. Figures can also be salvaged from otherwise hopelessly damaged Moss lamps, and stockpiled for use on a future Moss in need of help. The owners of Blue Flamingo, a California vintage lamp house, report success using this technique to restore Moss lamps in their personal collection. And, if this isn't possible (or you just don't like the figure on a particular lamp), 'mix-and-match' is always an option. Substitute a favorite figure from your own collection, one that comple-

ments the style of the lamp, for the missing or offending one. Mix-and-match is a time-honored tradition. After all, Moss did it."

A Few Random Notes

RADIO LAMPS. "Just because they don't start up right away, don't immediately assume the radios no longer work. Sometimes, those old tubes just take awhile to warm up!"

BRASS FITTINGS. "Cleaning the brass parts on Moss lamps can be tricky. Although some of the smaller brass fittings respond to polish, many of the larger pieces are just brass plated; if pitted or severely tarnished, they won't clean evenly. If the discoloration is really bothersome, there are metal shops that will replate the brass."

GENERAL CARE. "Make certain your Moss lamp is kept in surroundings that will preserve your diligent restoration efforts. Too much smoke, and the yellowy buildup will begin again. High wattage bulbs can cause spun glass shades to darken and droop. For showroom quality, exercise showroom care."

HOW TO DISPLAY THEM. "Moss lamps are shown off to their best advantage in uncramped, uncluttered surroundings, airy and open enough to give the lamps 'room to breathe'. A color scheme in solids will keep the focus on your lamps, particularly if the colors are such '50s favorites as pink, turquoise, black, or gold. The overall effect should be fresh and modern!"

Double Your Pleasure

"If you're feeling particularly ambitious and inspired, you can always make your own 'Moss lamp'. The prospect is not as daunting as it sounds, if you have access to lamp parts, household tools, the right adhesive (Craftics), and a source that will cut acrylic pieces to your specifications. An excellent source for 'how-to' information is *Cope's Plastics Book* by Dwight Cope. In addition to all the information you'll ever need to know about plastics, *Cope's Plastics* also includes photos, blueprints, and step-by-step instructions on how to make a variety of acrylic lamps. While your finished work may not be 'Moss' in actuality, it certainly will be in spirit: a fitting tribute to the unique vision that is the Moss heritage."

Thanks, Jeff! Those with additional questions about restoration, or other aspects of Moss lamps, can contact Jeff Bukas at 2714 N. Kimball, Chicago, IL 60647. (773) 486-3737.

The damage has begun: spun glass shade in need of a haircut (or at least a shot of spray starch!).

A spun glass shade sinks into the sunset. The original shape can sometimes be restored by applying a mixture of water and water-based glue.

When all else fails, recovering the shade frame with new or vintage material is an option, and the results can be as attractive as the original.

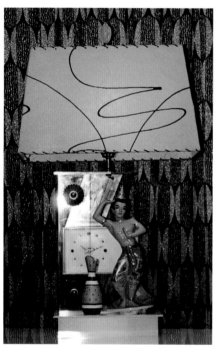

For lamps missing shades (or with shades beyond hope), period replacements can make things right again. Clock table lamp, #XT 815. *Photo by Heather Jeche. Courtesy of Richard A. Elioff*

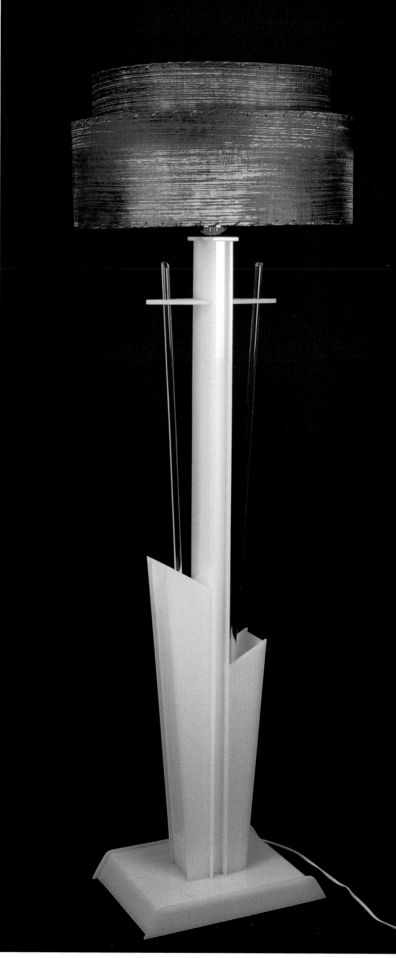

This replacement shade contrasts pleasingly with the white plexiglas lamp base. #X 2401, 4' 10" h. *Courtesy of Joe Anthony and Marie Christine Londrico*

Left: Its revolving days were long past, until a new motor and pin were installed in this example of #2310. If you can't cannibalize a working motor from another Moss lamp, check with a clock repair shop. Sometimes, clock parts can be adapted to restore the revolve function. *Johnson collection*

Right: A crack in the plexiglas? "Craftics Acrylic Solvent Cement" to the rescue! Any company that sells acrylic products should carry it.

When cleaning a Moss lamp, always use a product specifically designed for plastic and acrylics. Otherwise, scratching, clouding, or crazing can result. Figurines can be unbolted from their bases, and successfully cleaned with mild soap and water.

Feeling really ambitious? Break out the plexiglas, and create your own "Moss lamp". This floor model with birdcage, plus the wall clock, were designed and built by Moss collector and restoration expert Jeff Bukas, after careful perusal of *Cope's Plastics*. Floor lamp: 4' 4" h.; clock: 2' 6" h. *Courtesy of Jeff Bukas*

CHAPTER 7

"LIGHTING OUT FOR SAN FRANCISCO: A VISIT TO MOSS"

San Francisco (You've Got Me)

San Francisco has only one drawback—'tis hard to leave.

Rudyard Kipling

Rudyard had it right: San Francisco has plenty going for it. A shimmering skyline, with the Golden Gate emerging hazily through swirling fog, . . . a colorful and determined past, with the city rising victorious from the ruins of fire and earthquake, . . . a rich cultural diversity, which continues to attract tourists and transplants from around the world, . . . those "little cable cars", . . . that Tony Bennett song (and that Jeanette MacDonald one, too), . . . and, of course, Moss lamps.

Open Your Golden Gate

Moss Lighting finally closed up shop in the fall of 1997. In the fall of 1998, the company's remaining inventory was dispersed, and the building was sold. My visit was in the spring of 1998. I made it just in time.

Actually, if my purpose had been to see the original headquarters of Moss Manufacturing, I was over thirty years too late. That building, at 1124 Mission Street, fell to the wrecking ball in the early '60s. Since then, Moss Lighting has been located just one block away, at 1026 Mission.

On my visit, I first encountered the main floor lamp showroom, then in the process of being sold "to the bare walls". It was like many other such lighting display areas designed to appeal to today's discerning clientele: lots of crystal and European lamp stylings on view, but nary a trace of plexi. The third floor workshop, however, was another story. This was a journey back to an earlier era—one frozen, for the moment at least, in time.

Here, all the accouterments of Moss lamp construction were present and accounted for: the faithful "Shopsmith", waiting to cut a new batch of plexi into every shape imaginable, . . . the plexiglas panels themselves, some plain, others with embedded butterflies and gold threading, . . . boxes of gilded ceramic accent pieces and gleaming spinner motors, . . . spun glass shades, coated with their "secret formula", and all set for assign-

ment to just the right lamp, . . . birdcage frames and metal trim sections, ready to spring back into action. For the moment, it was possible to visualize this room as the hub of activity Moss Manufacturing had once been: a bubbling kettle of invention, with the skilled Moss staff bringing each new lamp idea to exuberant life. Memories of Thelma and Gerry Moss, Duke Smith, and John Disney were all around. And say—over in the corner—wasn't that where Terry the poodle used to dodge the air hose?

On the way out, I paid a visit to Mrs. Moss' office. By her desk, a #2295 floor lamp stood sentinel, the same ceramic "Comedy" and "Tragedy" faces I'd seen heaped in storeroom boxes now in their rightful positions. An oversize "Thelma" sign on the window ledge left no doubt as to whose base of operations this room had been and would always remain. And, in pride of place, there hung a painting of the *Thelma IV*, forever surging past the Golden Gate Bridge, facing bravely the headwinds of the future.

Above the Blue & Windy Sea

The Moss home, at 3299 Baker Street, is as much a part of the area's scenic beauty as is the Palace of Fine Arts park across the way. 3299's stately brick exterior seems as indigenous to Baker Street as the 1915 Panama-Pacific rotunda it faces. It's easy to imagine that obsessed Jimmy Stewart and enigmatic Kim Novak will soon stroll by, just as they once did in *Vertigo*.

Inside the Moss home, the decor embraces the future rather than the past. According to granddaughter Jori Slater Benjamin, Mrs. Moss always preferred "new" to "old". In other words, you have to search a bit to find the vintage Moss lamps! Using the "old" to create an artificial design concept called "modern" would seem incomprehensible to Thelma Moss. When her lamps were new, they were "new". . . but that was, after all, over forty years ago. Jay Benjamin recalls the first time he encountered an original Moss plexiglas lamp at an antique shop, purchased it, and proudly showed it to Mrs. Moss. Her response: "Where'd that old thing come from? You know, if I'd wanted one, I would have kept one."

Luckily, she did keep a few, including an exquisite clock table lamp, #X 3100, featuring the "Harlequinade" pair, and matching wall plaque, #X 5100. They blend in well with the Erté prints, crystal sculptures, and black lacquer accent pieces that comprise Mrs. Moss' most recent definition of "new". A true original fits in anywhere. Just ask Thelma Moss.

High on a Hill, It Calls to Me

We're en route now to Deovlet & Sons Furniture at 1660 Pine. It's rumored that Deovlet, serving the San Francisco community "since 1938", still has some of their old and unsold inventory in storage. Among the items viewed on a recent reconnaissance mission by Jay Benjamin was a suspected covey of Moss lamps.

Entering Deovlet & Sons is like entering a time capsule. Near the cash register and the "since 1938" sign hangs a photo, also evidently dating from 1938. The "& Son" of that photograph is the "Mr. Deovlet" of today. He looks exactly like his father. The current Mr. Deovlet points to a stairway leading to storage rooms on the upper floor. We move ahead, and our advance upward has all the excitement of an archeological expedition. What long-forgotten treasures await?

Into the storage jungle! Plunging past a herd of Heywood-Wakefield dinette sets and other atomic delights, we spot our quarry. Hidden in the furniture underbrush are—one, two, three—at least six Moss lamps! A 2273! A 2278! And, wonder of wonders, a pair of XT 816s, their deLee "Siamese Dancer" figures still posed acrobatically beneath several decades of dust. Deliverance at last!

The Pleasure of Her Company

March 22, 1999. Today is Thelma Moss' 91st birthday. Family, friends, (and one writer) have gathered to help her celebrate a long and eventful life. Mrs. Moss, as always elegantly turned out, samples a birthday candy and pronounces it good. Flattering mention of her past work brings a glimmer of amused approval. A cake is brought out, and Carol Moss Goodstein, who shares her mother's birthday, helps blow out the candles. There's applause and delighted laughter from all, including Mrs. Moss. She's in her element, clearly enjoying the company and the day. "Thelma Moss", says business associate Sid Bass, "was a dynamo." She still is.

Easily visible from Mission Street, the logo on the side of the Moss building, San Francisco. A bowl light below provides flattering evening illumination.

A step into the past: the Moss workshop, on the second floor of the 1026 Mission Street building, in 1998. According to staffers, the studio still looked much as it did when lamp production ended 30 years prior.

Top: Thelma Moss' office. The lamp, a favorite of Mrs. Moss, is #2295. 5' 1/2" h.

Bottom: Who's the boss? No question here!

Top right: Painting of the beloved *Thelma IV*, on the wall of Mrs. Moss' office.

Center right: The Moss home, just across from the Palace of Fine Arts, 3299 Baker Street, San Francisco.

Bottom right: The view from the front window of the Moss home: the Palace of Fine Arts. Last remaining remnant of the 1915 Panama-Pacific Exposition, the Palace rotunda is now the centerpiece of a scenic park. Both the Palace of Fine Arts (and the Moss home) can be glimpsed in the Hitchcock movie *Vertigo*.

Wall decor at 3299 Baker Street: Moss plaque #X 5100, again with the Lefton "Harlequinade" duo.

A clock lamp from the Moss home, featuring the Lefton "Harlequinade" pair. #X 3100

Detail, "Harlequinade" boy, Lefton #1379.

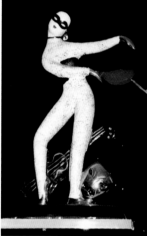

One-of-a-kind Moss lamp table, designed especially for the Moss home.

77

The hunt is on! Searching out unsold Moss inventory from the 1950s, rumored to be in storage at Deovlet & Sons Furniture, San Francisco.

Could it be? Yes, in the foreground it's Moss floor lamp #2273, waiting to be sprung from confinement.

#2273, released from captivity, and awaiting restoration.

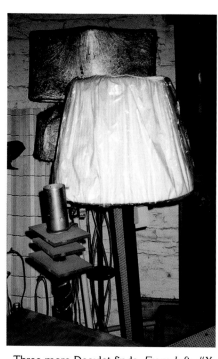

Original inventory photo of #2273.

Three more Deovlet finds. *From left:* #X 2402; # X 2403; #2278.

#X 2402 unearthed.

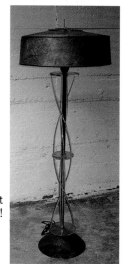

#X 2403, free at last!

Bottom center: #2278, reassembled with a Moss shade. The original price tags are still in place.

Bottom right: Inventory photo of #2278.

78

The catch of the day: table lamps #XT 816, with deLee Art "Siamese Dancers". Deovlet & Sons graciously presented the Moss family with the lamps found in storage, in recognition of the long and colorful history of Moss Lighting.

Always looking toward the future: Thelma Moss.

CHAPTER 8
"A RADIANT GALAXY OF MOSS TABLE LAMPS"

Some homes have one. Some have . . . well, more than that. In any event, the collectors of today have embraced the Moss lamps of the past. We're pleased to present, in living color, this galaxy of Moss table lamps, newly photographed, and loaned especially for the occasion by collectors nationwide. If original inventory photos exist, these have also been included, illustrating the changes that have taken place over the decades.

In the mid-'50s, retail prices for Moss table lamps began at $29.95, ranging to a high of $79.95 for the popular, fluorescent-stemmed #T 459, the table-sized "Leaning Lena". Today, they're a bit more than that. Heave a sigh for the good old days, restrain the envy, and . . . enjoy!

"Harlequinade" detail.

Inventory photo of #T 716, with different shade.

Lefton's "Harlequinade Boy" awaits his partner on #T 716. 2' 5" h.
Courtesy of Jeff Bukas

Nubian woman figurine on #XT 818. 2' 5" h. *Courtesy of Jeff Bukas*

Hedi Schoop's "Young China" musician, on #XT 813, with original shade. *Photo courtesy of Ken Paruti*

"Mambo" herself, in the inventory photo for #T 722.

"Mambo's" partner, "Mr. Mambo", on #T 722 (with different shade). 3' 1" h. *Courtesy of Joe Anthony and Marie Christine Londrico*

Decoramic "Bali Dancer", surrounded by starburst bulb covers, on #XT 819. 2' 10" h. *Courtesy of Joe Anthony and Marie Christine Londrico*

Unidentified medieval figure with mandolin. #XT 820, 3' h. *Courtesy of Jeff Bukas*

Detail, Egyptian woman.

An Egyptian woman strikes a traditional pose on #XT 821. 2' 8" h. *Courtesy of Jeff Bukas*

A change of clothes in ancient Egypt. #XT 821. *Photo by Heather Jeche. Courtesy of Richard A. Elioff*

#T 690, woman carrying two lanterns. The figurine is similar to those created by Jean Manley. According to the 1961 catalog, a male partner was also available. 2' 7-1/2" h. *Photo courtesy of William J. Burke*

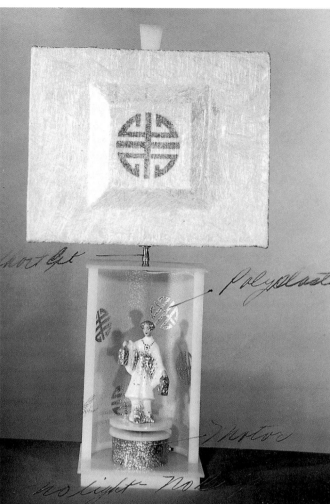

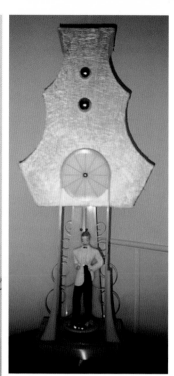

The popular "Escort" for "Prom Girl", "Cocktail Girl", and "Marilyn", here waiting for one of his dates on #T 740. 3' 7" h. *Photo courtesy of William J. Burke*

And here he is! Inventory photo, #T 690.

"Lantern Man" by Hedi Schoop on #XT 808. 2' 8" h. *Photo courtesy of William J. Burke*

Joining him, "Lantern Woman", #XT 808. *Photo courtesy of William J. Burke*

Hedi Schoop's "Poodle Girl" shows up again, this time on #XT 822. 2' 11" h. *Courtesy of Jeff Bukas*

A limber dance pair warms up on #XT 824. The oversize couple are themselves 19" h. Overall lamp height: 2' 9". *Courtesy of Jeff Bukas*

An unidentified dancer takes flight against a turquoise cloud. #XT 823. 2' 10" h. *Photo courtesy of William J. Burke*

85

A red-garbed guard stands ready to strike a metal gong on #XT 825. 2' 2" h. *Photo by Heather Jeche. Courtesy of Richard A. Elioff*

Detail, fabric shade

A turbaned man with scimitar stand watch on #XT 826 The fabric shade with an unusual oriental motif completes the scene. 2' 7" h. *Courtesy of Jeff Bukas*

Hedi Schoop "Phantasy"
planters pose gracefully on
#XT 807. Each, 2' 5-1/2" h.
*Courtesy of Joe Anthony and
Marie Christine Londrico*

All by herself: one-half of the
#XT 807 "Phantasy" pair.

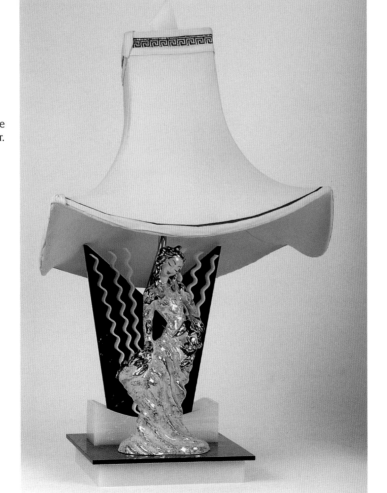

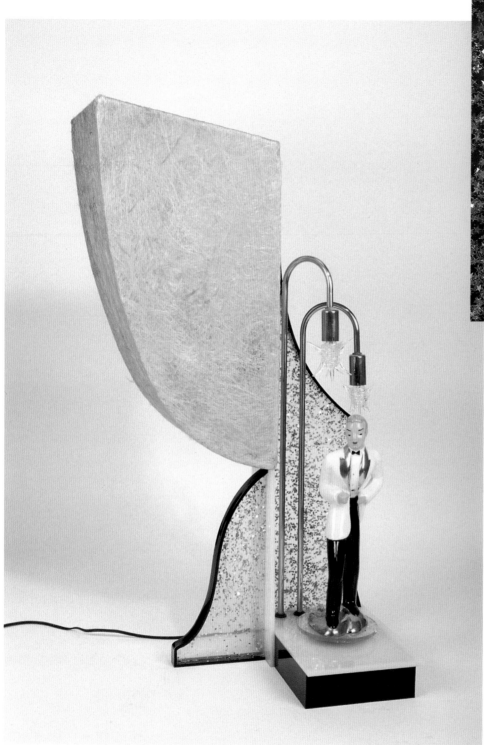

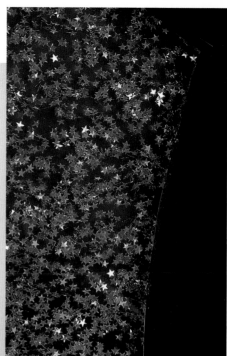

Detail, #XT 827's star plexi.

Opposite page:
Here's to exotic pets: woman with leashed panther on #XT 828. 2' 7" h. *Courtesy of Jeff Bukas*

Inset: Or, you can always opt for a dragon! #XT 854, 2' 3" h. *Photo courtesy of William J. Burke*

The Decoramic "Escort", spotlighted by star globes and backed by a torchiere-style shade. #XT 827, 2' 8" h. *Courtesy of Jeff Bukas*

#XT 827's mirror image, featuring "Marilyn". *Photo courtesy of William J. Burke*

Kneeling woman in gold gives a peaceful feeling to #XT 829. 1' 11" h. *Photo by Heather Jeche. Courtesy of Richard A. Elioff*

#XT 830: Oriental couple in black, under white silk fringed shades. The curlicue finials are a unique touch. Each, 2' 4" h. *Photo courtesy of William J. Burke*

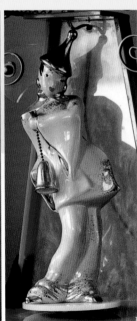

"Bell Girl" on blue plexi, #XT 803. 2' 8" h.

Detail, "Bell Girl".

Her partner, the Decoramic "Bell Boy".

Detail, "Bell Boy". *#XT 803 photos by Cheryl M. Gorski. Courtesy of Brenda Jackson Boyd*

DeLee Art's "Siamese Dancer"
man on #T 476. 2' 9" h. *Courtesy
of Jeff Bukas*

#T 476 with female "Siamese
Dancer". *Courtesy of Jeff Bukas*

91

So that's what he looks like! The "Bali Dancer" and her drum-playing companion feel the beat on #XT 831. (Judging by the rather generalized detail, these are the Decoramic Kilns, rather than Yona, versions of the "Bali" pair.) Each, 2' 10-1/2" h. *Courtesy of Joe Anthony and Marie Christine Londrico*

The same "Bali" figures, as interpreted by Yona, on another #XT 831 pair. *Courtesy of Joe Anthony and Marie Christine Londrico*

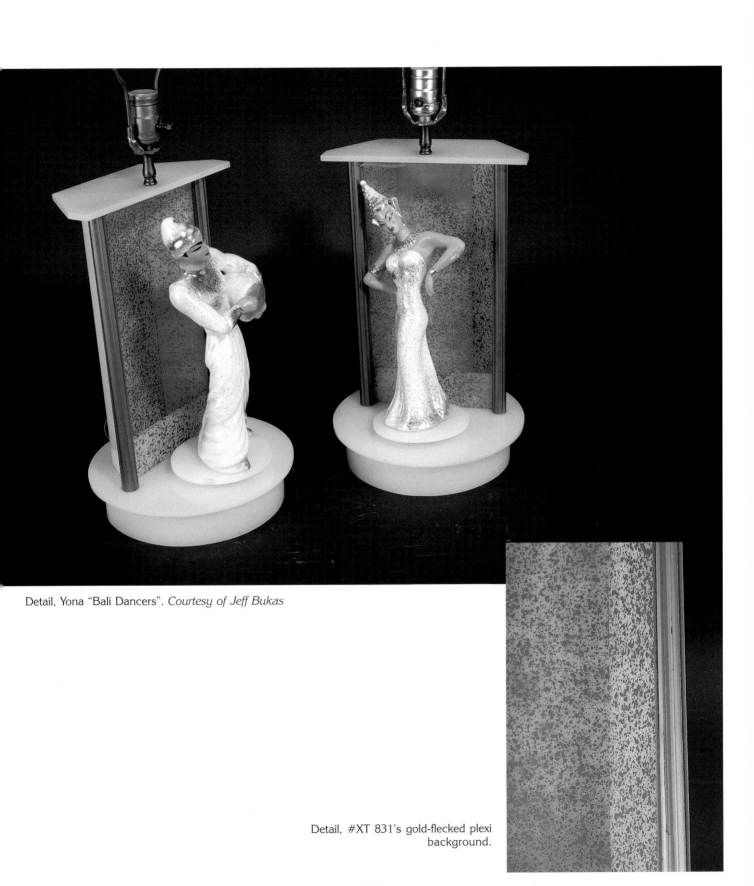

Detail, Yona "Bali Dancers". *Courtesy of Jeff Bukas*

Detail, #XT 831's gold-flecked plexi background.

#T 731 places Decoramic's "Prom Girl" center stage, with pebble-glass plexi panels supporting the shade. 3' 7-1/2" h. *Courtesy of Jeff Bukas*

As this original inventory photo indicates, "Prom Girl's" "Escort" could be posed patiently nearby. Usually, however, he was found on a #T 731 all his own.

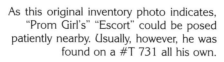

Decoramic
"Oriental" pair,
#T 638. The
scrim-like shades
are original. Each,
2' 6-1/2" h. *Photo
courtesy of
William J. Burke*

Inventory photo of #T 638 with
spun glass shade.

"Oriental Boy"
again, this time on a
more elaborate
stepped platform.
#T 633, 2' 6" h.

Detail, "Oriental Boy".

Bottom center; Detail, "Oriental Girl".
#T 633 photos, Johnson collection

Bottom right: Inventory photo, #T 633.

"Oriental Girl",
#T 633

95

Decoramic "Rhumba Woman" against plaid plexi background, with asymmetrical spun glass shade. #XT 834, 2' 11" h. *Courtesy of Jeff Bukas*

Not every man can wear pink. This one does, as he lounges against a piece of clear plexi. #XT 833, 2' 9" h. *Courtesy of Jeff Bukas*

Detail, spun glass shade.

#T 617. Here, "Rhumba Woman" goes into her dance in a cafe setting, complete with cocktail table and starlite lamp post. 2' 9-1/2" h.

Babalu! And here's "Rhumba Man", playing the same room.

Detail, "Rhumba Man". *#T 617 photos courtesy of Jeff Bukas*

Black unglazed figurines with gold luster trim add drama to # XT
835. The artificial flowers are the originals provided with the lamps.
3' h. *Courtesy of Joe Anthony and Marie Christine Londrico*

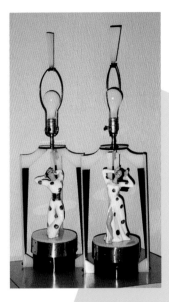

Polka-dot dancers on revolving pedestals, #XT 857. Each, 2' 11" h. *Courtesy of Jeff Bukas*

Bottom left: Brighten the corner where you are with this Moss "corner lamp", #T 712. The perforated brass center column is illuminated, as are the three hanging pod shades. 3' 3-1/2" h.

Bottom center: #T 712 detail. *#T 712 photos by Cheryl M. Gorski. Courtesy of Brenda Jackson Boyd*

Bottom right: #T 712 in original inventory photo.

Another corner lamp, #T 544, with triple torch pod shades and Decoramic "Bell Girl". 2' 10" h. *Courtesy of Joe Anthony and Marie Christine Londrico*

Here, the damaged original shades of #T 544 have been replaced with new ones fashioned of Japanese paper by the owner. 3' 6" h. *Courtesy of Jeff Bukas*

#XT 836. In this corner, "Cocktail Girl" reigns supreme. The mottled texture of her gown is a unique touch. 3' 6" h. *Courtesy of Joe Anthony and Marie Christine Londrico*

Move over, maracas girl! #XT 837, with the "Bell Boy" instead. Figurine mix-and-match was a regular occurrence in the Moss line, and today's collectors often replace damaged or missing lamp figures with a personal favorite. *Photo courtesy of William J. Burke*

Las maracas! Latin lady shakes it up, below two pod shades on #XT 837. 3' 8" h. *Courtesy of Jeff Bukas*

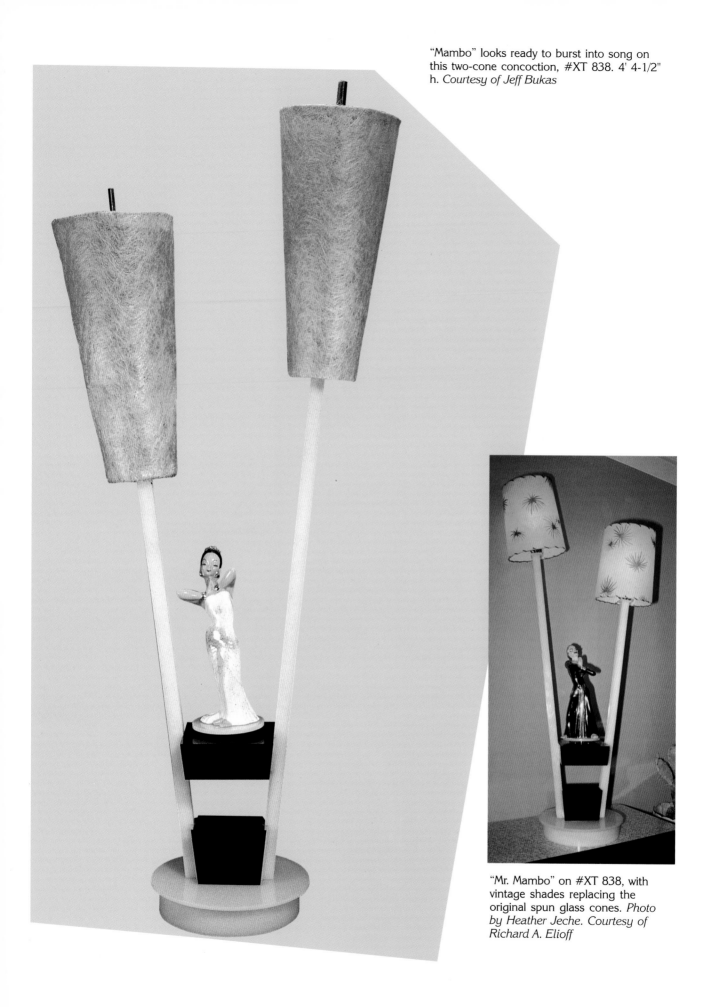

"Mambo" looks ready to burst into song on this two-cone concoction, #XT 838. 4' 4-1/2" h. *Courtesy of Jeff Bukas*

"Mr. Mambo" on #XT 838, with vintage shades replacing the original spun glass cones. *Photo by Heather Jeche. Courtesy of Richard A. Elioff*

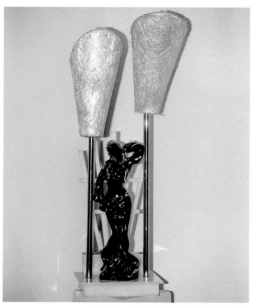

Black and gold pin-up girl basks before a trellis on #XT 839. 2' 8" h. *Photo by Heather Jeche. Courtesy of Richard A. Elioff*

Detail, Pin-up girl.

Horizontal cone shades are an arresting addition to #XT 840. Decoramic's "Ballet Dancers" are featured on the pair. Each, 3' 3" h. *Courtesy of Jeff Bukas*

Understated elegance: #XT 832, cylindrical spun glass shades on plexiglas platforms, from the Moss home in San Francisco.

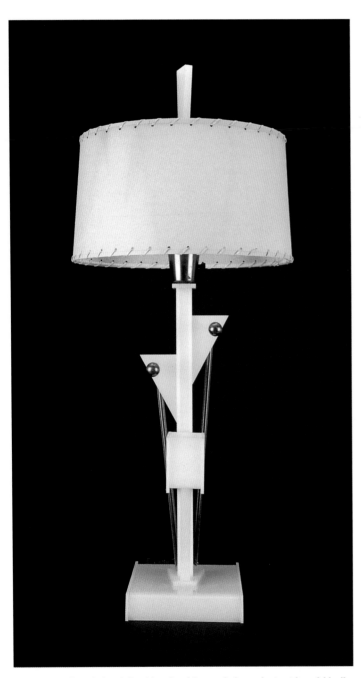

Attractively subdued (for Moss): white and clear plexi, with gold ball accents. #XT 841, 2'-6" h. *Courtesy of Jeff Bukas*

Side view of #XT 841.

A cloche-like fringed shade tops off #XT 842. 3' 5" h. *Courtesy of Jeff Bukas*

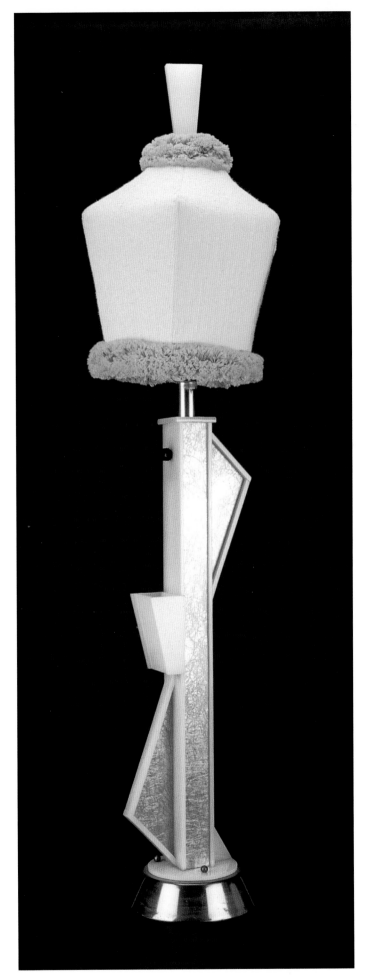

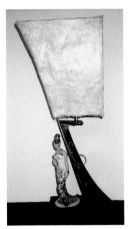

"Cocktail Girl" on an interesting angled lamp. The angle of the shade follows the line of the lamp stem. #XT 843, 3' h. *Photo courtesy of William J. Burke*

#XT 844: a pair of angled black plexi lamps. Here, the effect is achieved by the positioning of plexiglas pieces, rather than through the addition of other decorative elements. #XT 844 is the table version of floor model #2235. Each, 2' 6" h. *Photo courtesy of Amy Paliwoda*

Gold, black, and white plexi effectively combine in #XT 845. Each, 2' 5" h. *Courtesy of Jeff Bukas*

#XT 846, the table version of #2314. Each, 3' h. *Courtesy of Jeff Bukas*

Back for an encore, the deLee Art "Siamese Dancers" accent angled white plexi. #XT 847, each 2' 10" h. *Courtesy of Joe Anthony and Marie Christine Londrico*

#T 569, hanging lantern in a "bird-cage" style. 2' 4" h. A floor version, #2318, is shown in Chapter 9. *Courtesy of Jeff Bukas*

#T569 in its original inventory incarnation.

#T 459, the table-size rendition of the "Leaning Lena". As with the floor model, a fluorescent tube illuminates the stem. 1' 10-1/2" h. *Courtesy of Jeff Bukas*

CHAPTER 9
"A SPARKLING ARRAY OF MOSS FLOOR LAMPS"

Ready to move up to the big leagues? This array of Moss floor lamps, also newly photographed, presents many favorites of the Moss line, including the grown-up version of the "Leaning Lena", #2293. Again, any available inventory photos have been included for easy reference. Retail prices at the time for this glittering assortment of Moss ingenuity were in the $120-150 range. Reason enough to long for a time machine!

#2293, here with a floral print fabric shade.
Courtesy of Jeff Bukas

The best-selling of all Moss floor lamps! #2293, the "Leaning Lena", given its nickname for obvious reasons. A fluorescent tube inside illuminates the stem, and the shade is a whopping 28" square. Lamp: 4' 7" h. overall.
Courtesy of Joe Anthony and Marie Christine Londrico

Detail, floral print shade.

Top: Detail of butterfly plexi panel.

Bottom: Spun glass shade detail, #2293.

Another "Leaning Lena", with a butterfly design on the plexi panel. *Courtesy of Jeff Bukas*

#2317, an elegantly angled floor model, with marble-patterned plexi panel, and the Decoramic "Cocktail Girl" awaiting her escort. 5' h. *Courtesy of Joe Anthony and Marie Christine Londrico*

Original inventory photo of #2317.

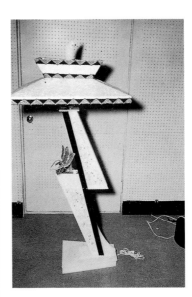

A different shade sets off the original inventory photo of #2306.

#2306, with fluorescent tubes in both of the angled stems. 5' h. *Courtesy of Joe Anthony and Marie Christine Londrico*

Sometimes the spun glass shades were painted, for a striking added effect. Here #2310 boasts an enormous 28" red fringed shade. The figurine is Decoramic Kilns' "Mr. Mambo". 5' h. *Courtesy of Joe Anthony and Marie Christine Londrico*

Inventory photo of #2310, with horizontal shade and "Mambo".

Another extreme fabric shade tops off the original inventory photo of #2249.

#2249 is unusual in that the base is of wood rather than plexiglas. The period shade is parchment. 5' 3-1/2" h. *Courtesy of Jeff Bukas*

#2314 as it appeared in inventory, with spun glass shade and crescent finial.

Starburst bulbs and glitter plexi panel highlight #2314. The fringed shade is not original. 5' h.
Courtesy of Jeff Bukas

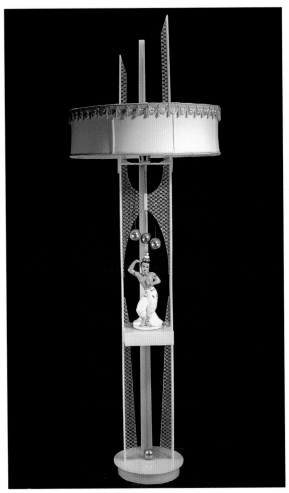

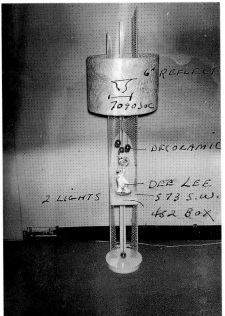

The female "Siamese Dancer" appears in the original inventory photo of #2345.

deLee Art's "Siamese Dancer" man is the focus of this sleek design, #2345. Columns extend beyond the shade to give the illusion of three finials. 6' h.
Courtesy of Jeff Bukas

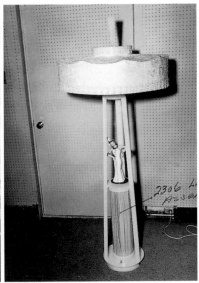
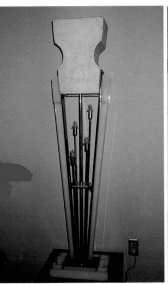
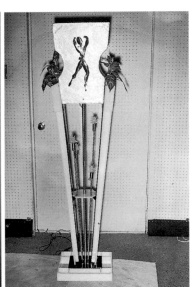
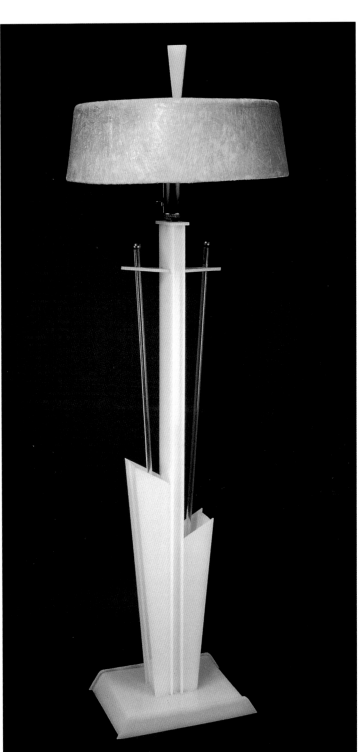

Top left: Decoramic's "Ballet Man" is the focal point of #2354. The center column contains a fluorescent tube and the spun glass shade is original. 4' 10" h. *Photo courtesy of David Meyer, Pleasure To Measure Custom Sewing*

Top center: Is she Yona's "Bali Dancer" or a Decoramic double? Either way, she's featured in the original inventory photo of #2354, as well as in the 1961 catalog.

Center left: Side planters flank the out-of-the-ordinary shade on floor model #2312. The original shade decoration is missing. 5' 4" h. *Courtesy of Jeff Bukas*

Center: Inventory photo of #2312 with shade decoration in place (and planters filled).

Angled plexi pieces give an oriental flavor to #X 2405. 4' 8" h. *Courtesy of Jeff Bukas*

#X 2401, a simple yet effective design in white and clear plexi, with original shade. (#X 2401, with period replacement shade, also appears in Chapter 6.) 5' 3" h. *Courtesy of Jeff Bukas*

113

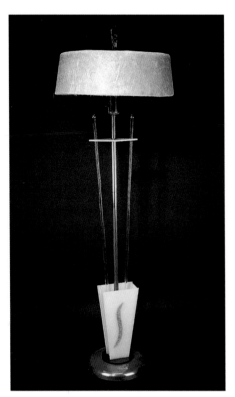

Another classic look (plus an extra-large planter) on a metal base. #X 2406, 5' 2" h. *Courtesy of Jeff Bukas*

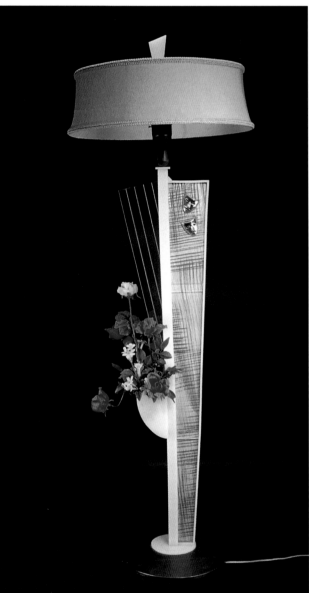

A mainstay of the Moss floor line, and a favorite of many, including Thelma Moss. #2295, 5' 5" h. *Courtesy of Jeff Bukas*

Inventory photo of #2295, with original spun glass shade.

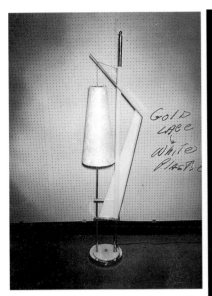

#2334 in its original inventory photo. An alternate version in black plexi, #2335, was also available.

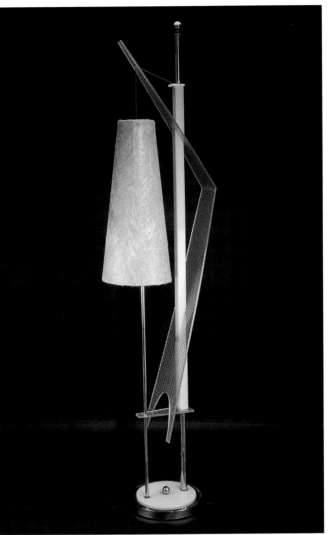

A suspended cone shade and angled gold lace plexi are the hallmarks of #2334. 5' 8" h. *Courtesy of Jeff Bukas*

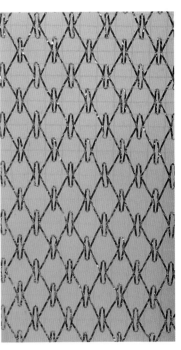

Detail, gold lace plexi.

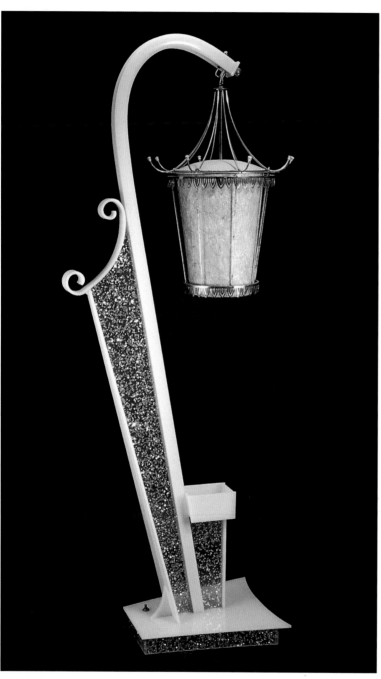

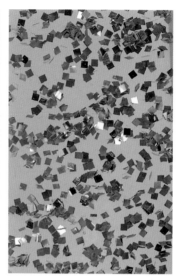

Detail of #2318's plexiglas sequin design.

Inventory photo of #2318. The birdcage frame is identified as the product of "Ideal Wire Works".

A birdcage-style hanging lantern distinguishes #2318. 5' 1" h. *Courtesy of Jeff Bukas*

A towering floor tree, #2328, with three red pagoda shades. 6' 5-1/2" h. *Courtesy of Jeff Bukas*

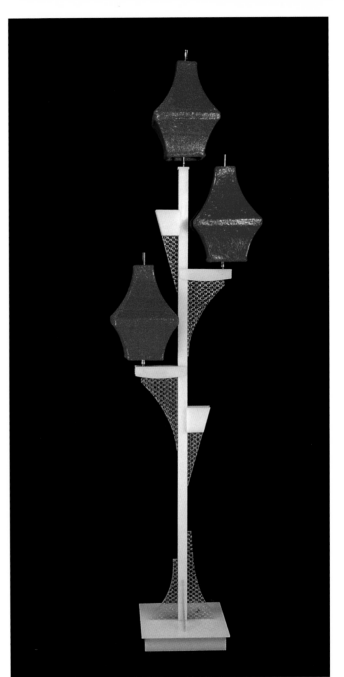

Similar design elements link this double cone pair from the Moss home. Table model #XT 817; floor model #X 2407.

#2328, as it appeared in inventory, with shades yet to be painted.

Coming Up Next . . .

Chapter 10 is a reprint, in its entirety, of *The 1961 Moss Lamps Catalog (#15)*. This detailed look at the Moss line for '61 is the only complete company catalog still known to exist. Then, with the spotlight shining on pure, unadulterated Moss, Part II of *Moss Lamps* plunges headlong into the black-and-white Moss inventory. These assembly reference photos, many complete with worknotes, provide a wish list that should keep the avid Moss collector on the prowl for years to come. Lights . . . camera . . . action! Presenting: The Moss Lamps Inventory!

Moss lamps are true "conversation pieces", with original designs, unique styling, and fascinating combinations of textures and colors.

Moss advertising flyer, 1958

Really, Moss lamps were ahead of their time.

Jori Slater Benjamin

117

Details of above lamp appear on inside cover.

presenting LAMPS BY

**MOSS of CALIFORNIA
& THE TAMI COLLECTION BY MOSS**

Catalog No. 15

No. T725 Table Lamp (on cover)

29 in. ceramic figurine in iridescent bronze lustre or white with gold trim, mounted on illuminated base of brass perforated metal and black trim and planter boxes. Back center column supports the 4 lantern shades. Illuminated base under figurine has separate switch. 4 polished brass lanterns.

Overall Ht. 62½ in.   Shade Size 9x5 in.

Note: Orders consisting of three or less items (lamps, clocks, tables, etc.) are subject to $1.50 packing charge for each item.

HOW TO ORDER FROM YOUR MOSS CATALOG!

1. PLEASE SPECIFY COLORS CLEARLY TO AVOID DELAYS.

   (a) Color of shade and trim.
   (b) Color of figurine or base, if ceramic.

2. WHEN ORDERING PAIRS OF LAMPS.

   If two lamps of one number are ordered, we send a pair unless otherwise specified. Most, but not all, are available in pairs.

3. WHEN ORDERING SINGLE LAMP.

   Be sure to state Male or Female figurines, Right or Left.

MOSS OF CALIFORNIA

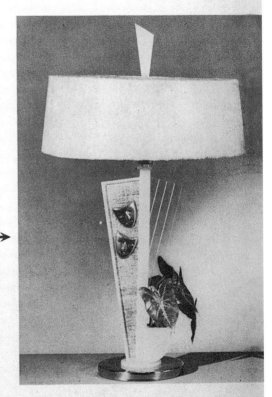

No. T459 Table Lamp

White plastic with black plastic back. All plastic base. Fluorescent tube inside illuminates stem. Separate switch. Pairs, Rights and Lefts. Spun glass shade in white, pink, gold, chartreuse, white with gold speckle, gold with black speckle. Trim: boucle, grey, black, gold.
Overall Ht. 30 in.
       Shade Size 22½ in. square.

No. T474 Table Lamp

White and clear plastic with poly-plastic inserts and 2 gold ceramic masks on brass base. Pairs, Rights and Lefts. Spun glass shade in white, pink, gold, chartreuse, white with gold speckle, gold with black speckle.
Overall Ht. 27 in.
       Shade Size 18x7 in. deep.

MOSS MANUFACTURING COMPANY, INC.
1124 Mission Street ● San Francisco 3, California
Telephone UNderhill 1-3040

No. T 476 Table Lamp

Ceramic figurine in pink, grey and gold, or white and gold on white plastic base. Figurine revolves. Electric Motor is UL approved, needs no oiling. Separate switch. Light in base, separate switch. Pairs, Male and Female. Spun glass shade in white, pink, gold, chartreuse, white with gold speckle, gold with black speckle. Shade Trim: Grey and gold, black and gold, white and gold, pink and gold.
Overall Ht. 30 in.
Shade Size 25x19½ x13 in. deep.

No. T 534 Table Lamp

Ceramic dancers in black, gold and white, revolving on white plastic base. Music box, cord operated and gold ceramic masks. Light in base has separate switch. Motor is UL approved, needs no oiling. Pairs, Rights and Lefts. Spun glass shade in white, pink, gold, chartreuse, white with gold speckle, gold with black speckle. Gold ceramic masks.
Overall Ht. 29 in.
Shade Size 22½ x12x13 in. wide.

MOSS OF CALIFORNIA

No. T 543 Table Lamp

Ceramic figurine in turquoise and gold; or black and gold; or white and gold, revolves on white plastic base. Scored clear plastic oriental screen background, with brass lamp posts and starry bulbs. Light in base has separate switch. Motor is UL approved, needs no oiling. Pairs, Male and Female. Spun glass shade in white, pink, gold, chartreuse, white with gold speckle, gold with black speckle. 3 brass discs.
Overall Ht. 30 in.   Shade Size 18½ x13 in. deep.

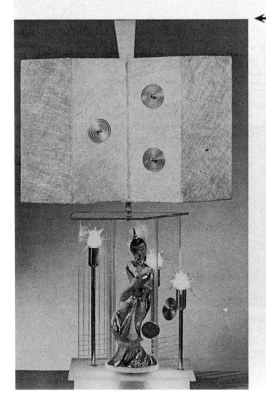

No. T 544 Corner Table Lamp

Ceramic figurine in black and gold; white and gold; turquoise and gold; revolves on white plastic base. Black and white polyplastic background with brass wire trim. Light in base has separate switch. Motor is UL approved, needs no oiling. Figurine available in Male and Female. Spun glass shades in white, pink, gold, chartreuse, white with gold speckle, gold with black speckle. No trim.
Overall Ht. 34 in.
Shade Size 14x10 in. deep.

Page 1

120

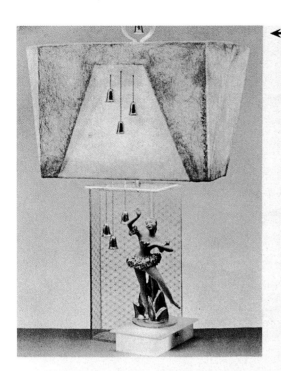

No. T578 Table Lamp

White plastic with gold lace plastic background. Ceramic figurine in terra cotta and gold, mat black and gold, revolves on white plastic base that is illuminated. Motor is UL approved, needs no oiling. Light in base separate three-way switch. Pairs, Male and Female. Spun glass shade in white, pink, gold, chartreuse, white with gold speckle, gold with black speckle. Three gold ceramic balls.
Overall Ht. 34 in.
Shade Size 22 ¼ x15x13 in. deep.

No. T579 Table Lamp →

Grey, white and gold or pink, white and gold ceramic figurine revolving on white plastic illuminated base. Two columns of silver glitter plastic with gold ceramic balls. Motor is UL approved, needs no oiling. Separate three-way switch in base. Pairs, Male and Female. Spun glass shade in white, pink, gold, chartreuse, white with gold speckle, gold with black speckle. No trim.
Overall Ht. 50 in.
Shade Size 8x18½ x13 in. deep.

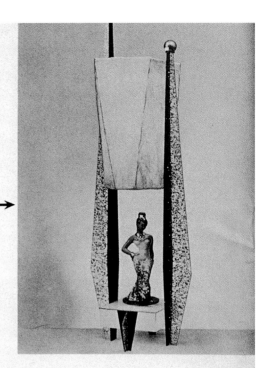

MOSS OF CALIFORNIA

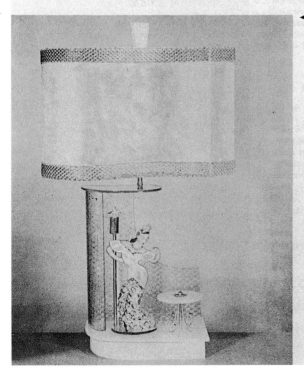

← No. T617 Table Lamp

White and gold or black and gold ceramic figurine revolves on white plastic base. Gold lace plastic background with starlite lamp post and small cafe table. Light in base, separate switch. Motor is UL approved and needs no oiling. Pairs, Male and Female. Spun glass shade in white, pink, gold, chartreuse, white with gold speckle, gold with black speckle. Gold metallic braid.
Overall Ht. 33½ in.   Shade Size 20½ x14x12 in. wide.

↑ No. 1 Aquarium Cocktail Table

Removable plastic planter trough on either side. Three plastic spreaders provide 1¾ in. of air space between aquarium and glass top. Entire table all plastic except glass top. Top glass ¼ in. plate, 50 in. long x 26 in. wide. Fluroescent tube under aquarium with outside switch.
Overall Ht. 16 in.   Plastic Aquarium Size 36x13½ in. wide.

Page 2

No. T633 Table Lamp

White and gold ceramic figurine revolves on black and white plastic base with white mesh plastic background and four gold plastic teardrops for trim. Revolving figure operates off separate switch. Motor is UL approved and needs no oiling. Pairs, Male and Female. Spun glass shade in white, gold, pink, chartreuse, white with gold speckle, gold with black speckle. Four gold plastic teardrops.
Overall Ht. 30 in.
Shade Size 18 x 13 x 10 in. wide.

No. T634 Table Lamp

Black, white and gold ceramic figure revolves on black and white plastic base with white mesh plastic background and gold and black polyplastic trim. Revolving figure operates off of separate switch. Motor UL approved and needs no oiling. Pairs, Male and Female. Spun glass shade in white, gold, pink, chartreuse, white with gold speckle, gold with black speckle. Two diamond shape plastic trims.
Overall Ht. 30 in.
Shade Size 22 x 13 x 12 in. wide.

MOSS OF CALIFORNIA

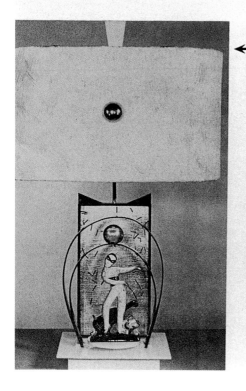

No. T635 Table Lamp

White, black and gold ceramic figurine revolves on white plastic base with gold and black polyplastic background, with double black plastic arch framing figure. Revolving figurine operates off of separate switch. Motor is UL approved and needs no oiling. Pairs, Male and Female. Spun glass shade in white, pink, gold, chartreuse, white with gold speckle, gold with black speckle. Gold ceramic ball trim.
Overall Ht. 29 in.
Shade Size 19½ x 12 x 11½ in. wide.

No. 7
Aquarium Cocktail Table

Aquarium is plastic with two fluorescent tubes under aquarium with outside switch. Four removable planters. Cut-away on aquarium provides for Fish to be fed without moving glass top and provides ample air space. Glass top.
Overall Ht. 15½ in.
Choice of 36 in. square or 38 in. round. Specify preference.

Page 3

122

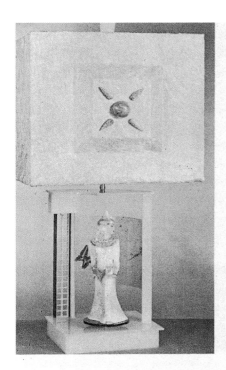

No. T 666 Table Lamp

White and gold, black and gold, ceramic figurine revolves on white plastic base with butterfly and gold fleck pattern plastic in background. Music box mounted on white mesh plastic with black plastic trim. Revolving figurine and light in base operate off separate switch. Motor is UL approved and needs no oiling. Pairs, Rights and Lefts, Male and Female. Spun glass shade in white, pink, gold, chartreuse, white with gold speckle, gold with black speckle. Gold ceramic ball with four gold plastic teardrops.
Overall Ht. 34 in.   Shade Size 18x16x11 in. wide.

No. T 667 Table Lamp →

White and gold, black and gold, ceramic figure revolves on black and white plastic base with gold lace plastic fence in background. Music box mounted underneath black and white plastic archway. Revolving figurine and light in base operate off separate switch. Motor is UL approved and needs no oiling. Pairs, Rights and Lefts, Male and Female. Spun glass shade in white, pink, gold, chartreuse, white with gold speckle, gold with black speckle. Metallic gold cord.
Overall Ht. 31½ in.

Shade Size 19½ x13x11 in. wide.

MOSS OF CALIFORNIA

No. T 684 Table Lamp

Two ceramic calypso figurines and illuminated platform revolve on white plastic base. Background of white louvered plastic with walnut plastic trim. Music Box mounted on side in white plastic, operated by pull cord. Figurine available in pumpkin hat, yellow jacket, brown body, white trousers with grey stripes. Light in base and light in platform. Lights and revolving figures operate off separate switch. Music box operates by pull cord. Motor is UL approved and needs no oiling. Pairs, Rights and Lefts. Spun glass shade in white, pink, gold, chartreuse, white with gold speckle and gold with black speckle. Brown and white or black and white trim.
Overall Ht. 34½ in.
Shade Size 23½ x14 in. deep.

No. T 688 Table Lamp →

Two walnut plastic leaf designs mounted on walnut plastic and brass base. Available in walnut, black or white plastic. Shipped in walnut if not specified. Three-way switch. Specify color. Pairs, Rights and Lefts. Spun glass shade in white, pink, gold, chartreuse, white with gold speckle and gold with black speckle.
Overall Ht. 29 in.   Shade Size 18x7 in. deep.

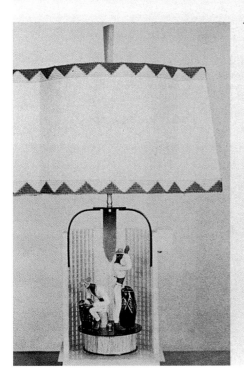

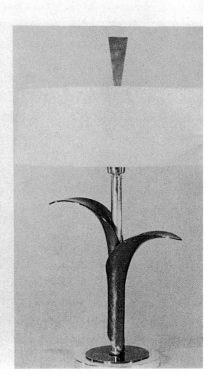

Page 4

← No. T 690 Table Lamp

White and gold, ceramic figure revolves on gold and white plastic base with white and gold vinyl plastic background. Revolving figurine operates off separate switch. Motor is UL approved and needs no oiling. Pairs, Male and Female. White spun shade with design in gold to match lamp background.
Overall Ht. 31½ in.
Shade Size 17¼ x14 in. high.

No. T 698 Table Lamp →

White and gold or black and gold ceramic figurines (very large, 19 in. tall) mounted on white plastic base with polished brass banding. Three white ceramic perforated balls containing individual light and shadowed in gold are suspended above figurines. Light in base and in each of three ceramic balls, separate switch. Hand-made shade of white silk shantung laminated over translucent vinyl with self trim and gold piping.
Overall Ht. 59 in.
Shade Size 20x24 in. deep.

MOSS OF CALIFORNIA

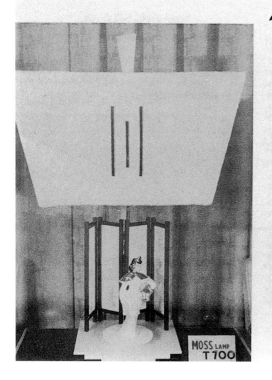

No. T 700 Table Lamp

Ceramic figure in white and gold or black and gold revolves on white plastic base with oriental leaf and butterfly screen effect in background. Revolving figurine operates off separate switch. Motor is UL approved and needs no oiling. Pairs, Male and Female. Spun glass shade in white, pink, gold, chartreuse, white with gold speckle, and gold with black speckle. Trimmed in black plastic.
Overall Ht. 39½ in.
Shade Size 19x11x12 in. deep.

No. T 712 Corner Table Lamp →

White and black or white and turquoise ceramic figurine revolves on black and white plastic base with three black plastic stems surrounding perforated brass column and supporting shades. Perforated brass column is illuminated. Separate three-way switch operates revolving figurine and light in brass column. Motor is UL approved and needs no oiling. Spun glass shade in white, pink, gold, chartreuse, white with gold speckle and gold with black speckle with satin finished brass shade tops.
Overall Ht. 39½ in.
Shade Size 11x6 in. high.

Page 5

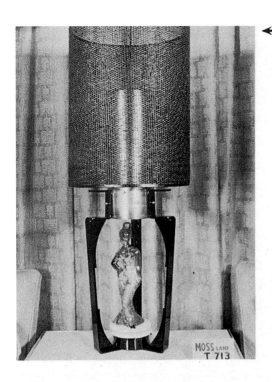

No. T 713 Table Lamp

Ceramic figurine in grey, white and gold or pink, white and gold, revolves on black and white plastic base with three black plastic columns supporting shades. Three-way switch. Revolving figurine has separate switch. Motor is UL approved and needs no oiling. Pairs, Male and Female. Inner shade of gold perforated metal with black woven outer shade.
Overall Ht. 40¼ in.
        Shade Size 14x20 in. high.

No. T 715 Table Lamp →

White and gold ceramic figurine revolves on black and white plastic base with white louvered plastic background. Metal trim on base matches that on shade. Revolving figurine operates off separate switch. Motor is UL approved and needs no oiling. Pairs, Right and Left, Male and Female. Spun glass shade in white, pink, gold, chartreuse, white with gold speckle or gold with black speckle, with metal buddha and circle trim.
Overall Ht. 30 in.
        Shade Size 18x10x14 in. deep.

MOSS OF CALIFORNIA

No. T 716 Table Lamp

Ceramic figurine in black, gold and white revolves on black plastic mounted on black and gold pedestal. Two black and gold columns support shade. Revolving figurine operates off separate switch. Motor is UL approved and needs no oiling. Pairs, Male and Female. Spun glass shade in white, pink, gold, chartreuse, white with gold speckle and gold with black speckle. Trimmed with black velvet design with gold center.
Overall Ht. 29 in.
        Shade Size 18x10x13 in. deep.

No. T 727 Table Lamp →

Two clear ice blue carved plastic arms mounted on brass pole and supporting shades. Three-way switch. Shade is two perforated brass cylinders circled in spiral fashion with clear ice blue plastic which is carved.
Overall Ht. 41 in.

No. T 726 Table Lamp

Brass perforated column with three carved plastic scrolls in clear ice blue. Column is illuminated. Operates off of special switch. White fabric shade laminated over translucent vinyl and trimmed with carved ice blue plastic band.
Overall Ht. 46 in.
        Shade Size 16x18x20 in. deep.

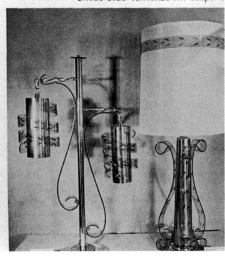

Page 6

No. T 731 Table Lamp

Ceramic figurine in white and gold revolves on white plastic base with two black columns with colored pebble glass inserts supporting shade. Light in base, separate switch. Motor is UL approved and needs no oiling. Pairs, Male and Female. White spun glass shade with unusual green and blue pebbled glass insert.
Overall Ht. 45 in.
  Shade Size 24x10 in. diameter.

No. T'732 Table Lamp →

Ceramic figurine in white and gold or purple and blue revolves on white and dark blue base with clear carved plastic background decorated with imported crystal prisms. Light in base, has separate switch. Motor is UL approved and needs no oiling. Pairs, Rights and Lefts, Female only. Spun glass shade in white, pink, gold, or white with gold speckle with lavender and gold trim.
Overall Ht. 34½ in.
  Shade Size 20x16x12 in. wide.

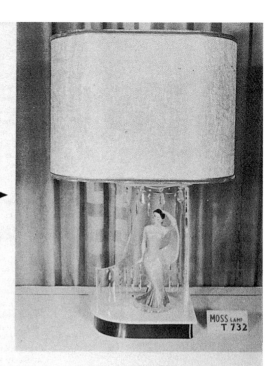

MOSS OF CALIFORNIA

No. T 733 Table Lamp

Ceramic figurine in white pearlescent revolves on white plastic base with gold carving on clear plastic column at side. Column is illuminated. Has special switch. Motor is UL approved and needs no oiling. Pairs, Rights and Lefts. Spun glass shade in white, pink, gold, chartreuse, white with gold speckle or gold with black speckle.
Overall Ht. 35 in.
  Shade Size 20x14x15½ in. high.

No. T 734 Table Lamp

Ceramic figurine in grey, white and gold or pink, white and gold revolves on white plastic base with curved clear carved plastic in background. Light in base. Has a special switch. Motor is UL approved and needs no oiling. Pairs, Male and Female. Spun glass shade in white, pink, gold, chartreuse, white with gold speckle or gold with black speckle. With gold rolled banding.
Overall Ht. 36 in.
  Shade Size 22x16½ in. deep.

No. T 735 Table Lamp →

Ceramic figurine in white and gold or black and gold revolves on white plastic base with illuminated carved tree design stemming from colored black and white pebbled glass plastic planter box and miniature lamp in background. Motor UL approved and needs no oiling. Light in base illuminates carved tree and separate light in miniature lamp. Pairs, Male and Female. Right and Left. Inner shade of white syn-skin and outer shade of gold mesh material with black velvet trim top and bottom.
Overall Ht. 35 in.
  Inner Shade Size 10x14x 6 in. wide.
  Outer Shade Size 18x16x11 in. wide.

Page 7

No. T 736 Table Lamp

Black and gold or white and gold ceramic figurine revolves on white plastic base with miniature table holding small planter with carved floral decoration. Side panel of black and white pebbled glass. Light in base illuminates background. Motor is UL approved and needs no oiling. Pairs, Rights and Lefts. Spun glass shade in white, pink, gold, chartreuse with center trim of black and white pebbled glass matching trim on base. Overall Ht. 35 in. Shade Size 18x16x11 in. wide.

No. T 737 Table Lamp

White, black and gold ceramic figurine revolves on white plastic base with clear scored plastic decor in background. Light in base, separate switch. Motor is UL approved and needs no oiling. Pairs, Male and Female. Rights and Lefts. Spun glass shade in white, pink, gold, chartreuse, white with gold speckle or gold with black speckle with clear scored plastic decorations matching base. Overall Ht. 37 in. Shade Size 20½x14x12 in. wide.

MOSS OF CALIFORNIA

No. T 738 Table Lamp

White plastic base with illuminated stem and planter box. Gold expanded metal on sides. Light in leaning stem has separate switch. Spun glass shade in white, pink, gold, chartreuse, white with gold speckle or gold with black speckle. Gold or black boucle shade trim.
Overall Ht. 31 in.
Shade Size 22 in. sq. x 8 in. deep.

No. T 739 Table Lamp

Black plastic with expanded metal sides illuminated by interior light within stem. Light in leaning column has separate switch. Spun glass shade in white, pink, gold, chartreuse, white with gold speckle or gold with black speckle. Trim in black and gold boucle.
Overall Ht. 54½ in.
Shade Size 22 in. sq. x 8 in. deep.

Page 8

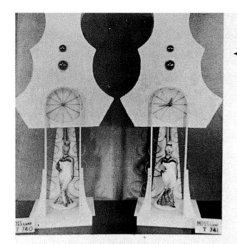

No. T741 Table Lamp

Ceramic figurine in white, grey and gold or pink, grey and gold revolves on white plastic base with curved plastic column supporting shade and electric clock with gold scrolls in background. Lamp has electric clock with sweep second hand. Motor UL approved and needs no oiling. Light in base, separate switch. Spun glass shade in white, pink, gold, chartreuse, white with gold speckle or gold with black speckle, with two half round balls, gold ceramic.
Overall Ht. 43 in.

Shade Size 18x23½x8 in. deep.

Note: T740 is companion lamp without electric clock. T741 has electric clock built in to shade.

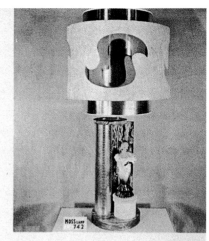

No. T740 Table Lamp

Ceramic figurine in white, grey, and gold or pink, grey and gold revolves on white plastic base with curved plastic column supporting shade and with gold scrolls in background. Motor UL approved and needs no oiling. Light in base, separate switch. Pairs, or may be used with T741 companion lamp with electric clock. Check price list for price of T741. Spun glass shade in white, pink, gold, chartreuse, white and gold speckle or gold with black speckle, with two half round balls, gold ceramic.
Overall Ht. 43 in.   Shade Size 18x23 ½ x8 in. deep.

No. T 742 Table Lamp

Ceramic figurine in purple, white and gold or black, white and gold revolves on a white plastic pedestal mounted on purple base with brush gold finish or black base with brush gold finish. Polished brass perforated column illuminates background. Revolving figure, separate switch. Motor UL approved and needs no oiling. Perforated column illuminates. Pairs, Male and Female. White spun glass outer shade with open design showing perforated gold foil inner shade. Specify color of figurine purple or black.
Overall Ht. 44 in.   Outer Shade 19½ x 14 in. deep.
                            Inner Shade 13½ x 20 in. deep.

MOSS OF CALIFORNIA

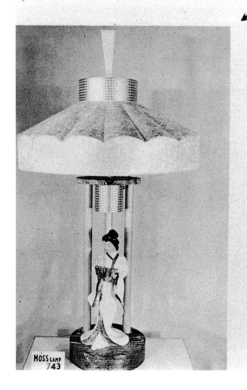

No. T 743 Table Lamp

Large (17 in.) ceramic oriental figure in white and gold or bronze lustre mounted on black base subdued by gold brush finish or white base with gold brush finish. Pairs, Rights and Lefts. Shadow light in cylinder above figurine which reflects on figure. Specify black or white. Spun glass shade in white, pink, gold, chartreuse, white with gold speckle or gold with black speckle. Metal trim at top.
Overall Ht. 41 in.
          Shade Size 24½ x12 in. deep.

No. T 744 Table Lamp

Ceramic figurine in white, black and gold revolves on black plastic base with clear diamond cut plastic screen and hanging lantern in background. Revolving figurine has separate switch. Motor UL approved and needs no oiling. Pairs, Male and Female. Spun glass shade in white, pink, gold, white with gold speckle or gold with black speckle.
Overall Ht. 34 in.
          Shade Size 18½ x16x10 in. wide.

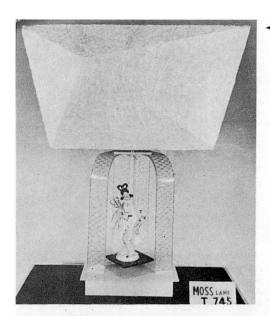

No. T 745 Table Lamp

White, black, and gold ceramic figurine revolves on white plastic base with two gold lace plastic archways. Revolving figurine has separate switch. Motor UL approved and needs no oiling. Pairs, Male and Female. Spun glass shade in white, pink, gold, chartreuse, white with gold speckle or gold with black speckle. Overall Ht. 29½ in.
Shade Size 22x13x9 in. wide.

No. T 746 Table Lamp

White and gold ceramic figurine revolves on white plastic base with clear diamond cut plastic background trimmed with gold metal leaves. Revolving figurine has separate switch. Motor UL approved and needs no oiling. Pairs, Rights and Lefts. Spun glass shade in white, pink, gold, chartreuse, white with gold speckle or gold with black speckle with gold leaf trim matching base. Overall Ht. 32 in.
Shade Size 19½ x 16 x 14 in. wide.

MOSS OF CALIFORNIA

No. T 747 Table Lamp

White and gold or black and gold ceramic figurine revolves on black and white illuminated base with gold expanded metal curved background. Revolving figurine and light in base have separate switch. Motor UL approved and needs no oiling. Pairs, Male and Female, Right and Left. Spun glass shade in white, pink, gold, white with gold speckle and gold with black speckle. Trim; black plastic and gold metal. Overall Ht. 32 in.
Shade Size 18 x 14 x 10 in. wide.

No. 2284 Floor Lamp

White plastic base with illuminated stem and planter box. Gold expanded metal on sides. Light in leaning stem, separate step switch at base. Spun glass shade in white, pink, gold, chartreuse, white with gold speckle or gold with black speckle. Gold or black boucle shade trim. Overall Ht. 55 in.
Shade Size 28 in. sq. x 10 in. deep.

Page 10

129

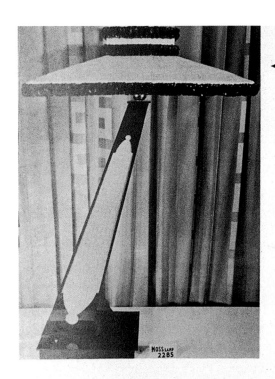

No. 2285 *Floor Lamp*

Black plastic with expanded metal sides illuminated by interior light within stem. Light in leaning column has separate switch. Spun glass shade in white, pink, gold, chartreuse, white and gold speckle or gold with black speckle. Trim in black and gold boucle.
Overall Ht. 54½ in.
Shade Size 28 in. sq. x 9½ in. deep.

No. 2293 *Floor Lamp*

White plastic with black plastic back. Fluorescent tube inside illuminates stem. Separate switch. Spun glass shade in white, pink, gold, chartreuse, white with gold speckle, gold with black speckle. Trim: black or gold boucle.
Overall Ht. 55 in.
Shade Size 28 in. square.

MOSS OF CALIFORNIA

No. 2295 *Floor Lamp*

White plastic with scored clear plastic trim. Gold ceramic masks mounted on polyplastic column. Brass base. Spun glass shade in white, pink, gold, chartreuse, white with gold speckle, gold with black speckle.
Overall Ht. 60½ in.
Shade Size 24x7 in. deep.

No. 2326

Hanging Lantern Floor to Ceiling Lamp

White plastic leaves with white plastic arms holding lantern-type shades. Three-way switch on column. Spun glass shade in white, pink, gold, chartreuse, white with gold speckle, gold with black speckle. Brass hanging lantern.
Shade Size 9½ x 12 in. deep.

Page 11

130

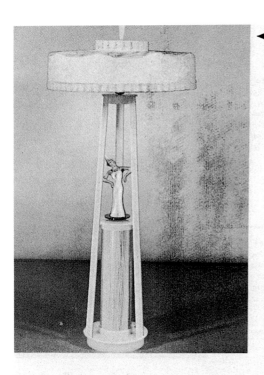

No. 2354 Floor Lamp

White and gold, black and gold, pink and gold ceramic figurine revolves on gold and white polyplastic column with three white plastic columns supporting shade. Fluorescent tube inside column illuminates stem. Revolving figurine and fluorescent tube operate off separate switch. Motor is UL approved and needs no oiling. Pairs, Male and Female. Spun glass shade in white, pink, gold, chartreuse, white with gold speckle, gold with black speckle. White and gold braid.
Overall Ht. 58 in.
    Shade Size 27x9 in. deep.

No. 2363 Floor Lamp ➡

Two plastic leaf designs mounted on plastic and brass base. Available in walnut, black or white plastic. Shipped in walnut plastic if not specified. Three-way switch. Specify color. Spun glass shade in white, pink, gold, chartreuse, white with gold speckle, gold with black speckle.
Overall Ht. 59 ½ in.
    Shade Size 24x7 in. deep.

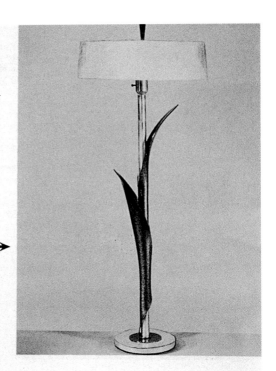

MOSS OF CALIFORNIA

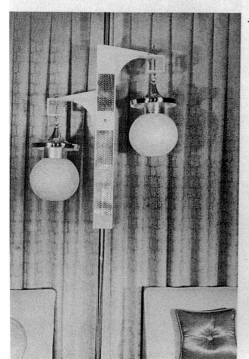

⬅ No. 2369 Floor to Ceiling Lamp

Pole – two spun glass balls with brass tops suspended from white plastic arms with perforated polished brass banding inset in center panel. Three-way switch. Standard height for 8' to 9' ceiling, extensions available; specify height. Spun glass shade in white, pink, gold, chartreuse, white with gold speckle or gold with black speckle. Polished brass top pieces.
Overall Width 29 in.
    Shade Size 10 in.

No. 2370 Floor to Ceiling Lamp ➡

Pole with two black plastic arms support louvered plastic shades. Indian brass trim. Three-way switch. Standard for 8' to 9' ceiling, extensions available, specify height. White louvered plastic shades with black plastic trim.
Overall Width 24 in.
    Shade Size 9 ½ x 11 in. deep.

Page 12

131

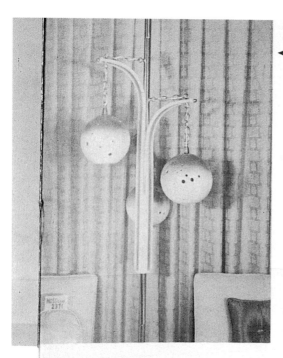

← **No. 2371** *Floor to Ceiling Lamp*
Pole – White plastic with brass band-
ring inset. Three-way switch.
Standard height for 8' to 9' ceiling,
extensions available, specify height.
Shades are white perforated ceramic
balls shaded with gold.
Width 22 in.   Shade Size 9 in. ball.

No. 2373 *Tree Lamp* →
Two crackle glass shades suspended
from black plastic arms supported by
brass tubing with antique mirror plastic inset. Three-way switch, step-on
type. Shade has crackle glass balls
with perforated brass cone inserts.
Overall Ht. 61 in.
          Shade Size 8 in. glass balls.

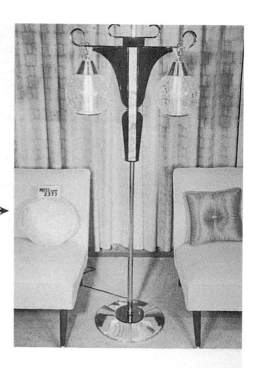

MOSS OF CALIFORNIA

← **No. 2376** *Tree Lamp*
Polished brass tubing supports three
white plastic columns combined with
decorative gold and black plastic,
from which three separate lights are
suspended. Lamp is trimmed with
three white plastic planter boxes.
Three-way step switch. Three 6 in.
white perforated ceramic balls with
polished brass shade tops.
Overall Ht. 65 in.

No. 2377 *Floor to Ceiling Lamp* →
Grey, white and gold or pink, white
and gold ceramic figurine revolves
on white plastic and expanded metal
brass base with three brass rods supporting upper part of lamp which
contains four gold perforated illuminated balls suspended from white
plastic arms. Expanded metal column
above figurine is illuminated.
Standard height for 8' to 9' ceiling,
extensions available, specify height.
Revolving figurine operates off separate switch. Motor is UL approved
and needs no oiling. Four perforated
4 ½ in. gold ceramic balls.
          Size 22 ¾ in. wide.

Page 13

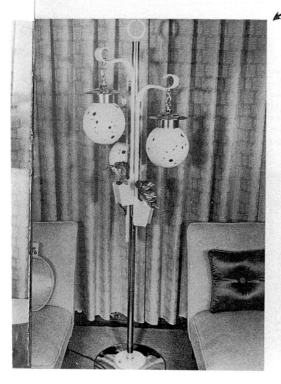

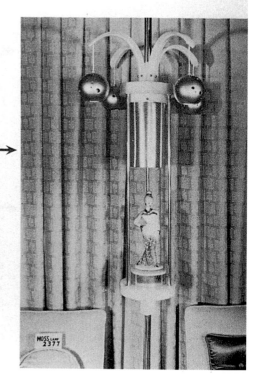

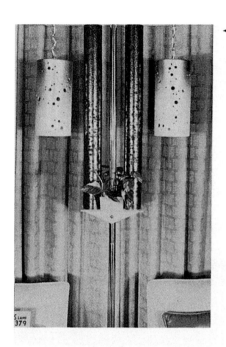

No. 2379 *Floor to Ceiling Lamp*

Two black and gold tortoise shell type columns with white plastic trim and planter box. Three-way switch. Standard height for 8' to 9' ceiling, extensions available, specify height. Shades are removable. Two white and gold ceramic shades.
Overall Width 26 in. wide.

Shade Size 6x13 in.

No. 2381 *Floor to Ceiling Lamp*

Four carved arms supporting shades are mounted on center pole of black and gold antique finish. Standard height for 8' to 9' ceiling, extensions available, specify height. Three-way switch. Four perforated polished brass lanterns.
Overal Width 26 in.

No. 2382 *Floor to Ceiling Lamp*

Three carved ice blue plastic arms mounted on brass pole from which shades are suspended by gold link chain. Standard height for 8' to 9' ceiling, extensions available, specify height. Three-way switch. Three perforated polished brass cylinders spiraled by clear ice blue carved plastic.
Overall Width 22 in.

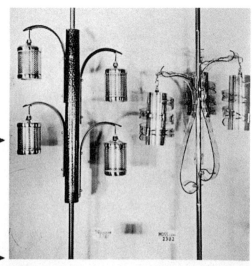

MOSS OF CALIFORNIA

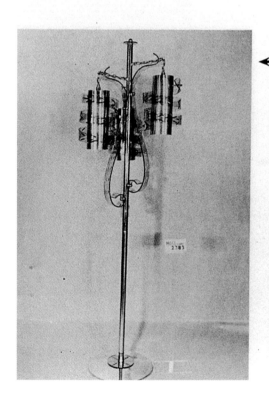

No. 2383 *Tree Lamp*

Three carved ice blue plastic arms mounted on brass pole from which shades are suspended by gold link chain. Three perforated polished brass cylinders spiraled by clear ice blue carved plastic.
Overall Ht. 72 in.

No. 2386 *Floor to Ceiling Lamp*

Two spun glass shades suspended by gold link chain from two white plastic leaves mounted on polished brass pole. Standard for 8' to 9' ceiling, extensions available, specify height. Spun glass shade in white, pink, gold, chartreuse, white with gold speckle or gold with black speckle.
Overall Ht. floor to ceiling.

Shade Size 14x8½ in.

No. 2387
Floor to Ceiling Lamp

Shades suspended from two black plastic curved arms with center design matching shades. Standard for 8' to 9' ceiling, extensions available, specify height. Outer shade black mesh, inner shade of polished brass with grated pattern.
Overall Ht. floor to ceiling.
Shade Size 11½ x 8 in.

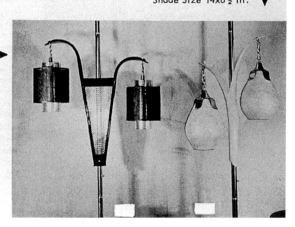

Page 14

133

← **No. 3018**
Wall Decorator with Pendulum Clock

White spun glass with black plastic trim and planter box. Clock has black plastic face, is 8-day wind with pendulum. No electric cord. Size 30x46 in. tall.

No. 3026 →
Wall Decorator with Pendulum Clock

White spun glass with gold chain design and black plastic planter box. Clock is black plastic with gold hands and gold lines indicating hour. Clock is 8-day wind with pendulum. No electric cord. Size 46 in. dia.

MOSS OF CALIFORNIA

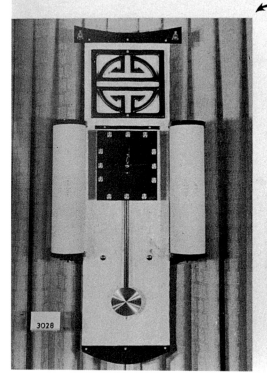

← **No. 3028**
Wall Decorator with Pendulum Clock

White spun glass with black plastic trim and black oriental ceramic tile design above clock. Two white plastic cylinder shades with gold oriental design on either side enclose lights which illuminate clock. Clock has black plastic face with polished brass oriental symbols representing numerals. Clock is 8-day wind with pendulum. Electric cord for lights is concealed by adjustable polished brass rod extending from bottom of wall piece. Size 23 in. wide, 55 in. height.

No. 3029 →
Wall Decorator with Pendulum Clock

White spun glass panel with black plastic and gold ceramic ball trim and black plastic planter boxes. Clock has gold scoring representing hours in combination with numerals 3, 6, 9, and 12. Clock has black plastic face and is 8-day wind with pendulum. No electric cord. Size 26 in. wide.
46½ in. height.

Page 15

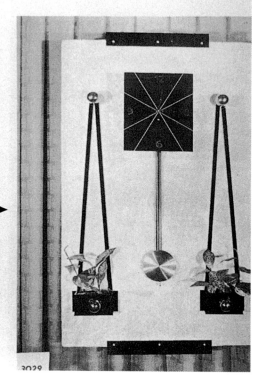

134

MOSS OF CALIFORNIA

← **No. 3030**

Wall Decorator with Pendulum Clock

Black, gold and red tortoise shell type background with black plastic trim and planter box. Clock has black plastic face and is 8-day wind with pendulum. Gold cord and tassels with satin brass rosettes decorate clock background. No electric cord to show.
Size 26x47 in. tall.

No. 3031
Wall Decorator with Pendulum Clock →

Black and gold tortoise shell type background with black plastic trim and planter box. Gold filigree design enhances background. Clock has black plastic face and is 8-day wind with pendulum.
Size 26x48 in. long.

THE TAMI COLLECTION BY MOSS

← **No. 11A Table Lamp**

Gold crackle ball trimmed with black. Hand-made shade in white nubby textured fabric, with wide black velvet piping, and narrow gold cording on each side.
Overall Ht. 54 ½ in.
    Shade Size 17x22 in. deep

No. 19A Table Lamp →

White and gold base with imported crystal prisms. Light in ceramic base illuminates crystal prisms. Operates off separate switch. Hand-made shade in white nubby fabric, rolled self trim, applied in scalloped effect and bounded on each side by gold cording. Gold cording trim also at bottom of shade.
Overall Ht. 48 ½ in.
    Shade Size 19x22 in. deep.

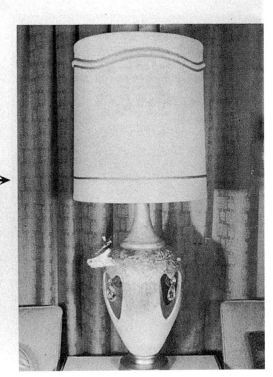

Page 16

No. 34 A Table Lamp

White and black ceramic base with gold metal floral design. Hand-made shade in white fabric textured with gold metallic threads, laminated over translucent vinyl, and with gold metal decorative floral design trim, matching that on base.
Overall Ht. 47 in.
　　　Shade Size 19x22 in. deep.

No. 50A Fireside Lamp

White with antique gold effect and metallic leaf trim matching that on shade. Hand-made shade in white textured fabric laminated over translucent vinyl with self-trim top and bottom and antique gold and white metallic leaf trim.
Overall Ht. 63 in.
　　　Shade Size 20x23 in. deep.

THE TAMI COLLECTION BY MOSS

No. 55 A Table Lamp

Ceramic base available in brown lustre with grey antique or white antiqued. Oriental scene. Hand-made shade in textured fabric laminated over translucent vinyl with matching trim.
Overall Ht. 46 in.
　　　Shade Size 18x21 in. deep.

No. 56A Table Lamp

White antiqued ceramic base with embossed oriental scene. Hand-made shade in white textured fabric laminated over translucent vinyl with black velvet and gold trim.
Overall Ht. 52 in.
　　　Shade Size 19x22 in. deep.

Page 17

← No. 57 A Table Lamp

Carved ceramic base in artistic white or green glaze mounted on satin brass base. Hand-made shade in white textured fabric laminated over translucent vinyl with gold braid.
Overall Ht. 48 in.
Shade Size 19x22 in. deep.

No. 61 A Table Lamp →

White antique ceramic base with smoke-grey antique handles, cap and base. Hand-made shade in white textured fabric laminated over translucent vinyl with matching rolled trim.
Overall Ht. 51 in.
Shade Size 19x22 in. deep.

THE TAMI COLLECTION BY MOSS

← No. 64 A Table Lamp

Ceramic base available in flowing jade green glaze or flowing rust and cinnamon glaze, mounted on antique gold and matching color base. Hand-made shade in white textured fabric laminated over translucent vinyl, matching color trim.
Overall Ht. 49-1/2 in.
Shade Size 18x22 in. deep.

No. 68 A Table Lamp →

Hand applied gold leaf ceramic base on antique gold with black pedestal. Available also in silver leaf but if not specified, gold will be sent. Shade: White textured fabric laminated over translucent vinyl with wide black velvet trim and gold cording.
Overall Ht. 45 in.
Shade Size 14x18x21 in. deep.

No. 69 A Table Lamp

Hand applied gold leaf floral design ceramic base on gold leaf sub base. Antiqued. Also available in silver leaf but gold leaf will be sent if not specified. Shade: White textured fabric laminated over translucent vinyl with narrow black edging.
Overall Ht. 44-1/2 in.
Shade Size 14x18x21 in. deep.

Page 18

137

No. 70A Table Lamp

Antiqued hand applied gold leaf ceramic base mounted on black teak finished sub base. Also available in silver leaf. If not specified, gold will be sent. Shade: White textured fabric laminated over translucent vinyl with self trim and gold banding at top and bottom.
Overall Ht. 51½ in.
    Shade Size 18x20x24 in. deep.

No. 71A Table Lamp

Antique hand applied gold leaf ceramic base mounted on black sub base. Also available in silver leaf but if not specified will be sent in gold. Shade: White textured fabric laminated over translucent vinyl with black banding top and bottom.
Overall Ht. 46 in.
    Shade Size 14x18x21 in. deep.

THE TAMI COLLECTION BY MOSS

72A Table Lamp

Drip glaze ceramic base in two tone brown, burnt orange or amethyst, hand applied gold leaf or silver leaf sub base. Specify ceramic color. Also specify sub base to be in gold or silver leaf or gold will be sent. Shade: Off white or beige nubby fabric laminated over translucent vinyl with harmonizing trim.
Overall Ht. 55 in.
    Shade Size 16x18x20 in. deep.

No. 74A Table Lamp

Ceramic base in lavender, deep brown or blue with iridescent gold luster finish. Sub base gold leaf. Specify color of ceramic. Also specify sub base to be in gold or silver leaf or gold leaf will be sent. Shade: White textured fabric laminated over translucent vinyl with trim to match ceramic base.
Overall Ht. 41 in.
    Shade Size 17x18x18 in. deep.

Page 19

138

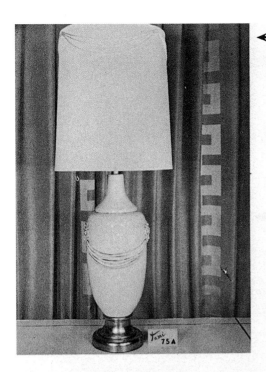

No. 75A Table Lamp

Antique white, avocado or morning-glory blue ceramic base mounted on hand applied gold or silver leaf base. Specify color of ceramic base. Also specify sub base to be in gold or silver leaf or gold leaf will be sent. Shade: White textured fabric laminated over translucent vinyl with white cord drape trim.
Overall Ht. 51 in.
    Shade Size 16x18x22 in. deep.

No. 76A Table Lamp

Ceramic base in white antique with gold leaf medallion and hand applied gold leaf sub base or hand applied gold leaf on entire lamp base or hand applied silver leaf on entire lamp base. Specify color. Shade: White textured fabric laminated over translucent vinyl with double band of white rolled trim spiraled with gold cording.
Overall Ht. 48 in.
    Shade Size 16x18x22 in. deep.

THE TAMI COLLECTION BY MOSS

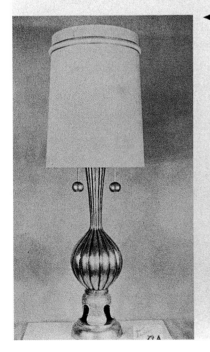

No. 79A Table Lamp

Gold leaf antiqued ceramic with silver leaf antiqued metal sub base, and gold leaf bottom base. Double light socket with pull cords. Gold leafed ceramic balls operate pull cords. Shade: Off white textured fabric with half-round self trim and gold cord.
Overall Ht. 50½ in.
    Shade Size 14x15½x22 in. deep.

No. 80A Table Lamp

Gold leafed base combined with silver leaf and terra cotta antiquing. Shade: White nubby fabric laminated over translucent vinyl. Shade trim in gold and white harmonizing with design on base.
Overall Ht. 50 in. Shade Size 14x16x22 in. deep.

No. 81A Table Lamp

Jade green ceramic with gold leaf antiqued bands and sub base. Shade: White textured fabric laminated over translucent vinyl with raised band of self trim.
Overall Ht. 45½ in.
    Shade Size 14x16x20 in. deep.

Page 20

139

No. 83A Table Lamp

White ceramic base with base top and under base of gold leaf with terra cotta antiquing. Mounted on black teak finished sub base. Shade: White textured fabric laminated over translucent vinyl with fine gold cord trim.
Overall Ht. 36 in.
Shade Size 13x16x18 in. deep.

No. 84A Table Lamp

Gold and silver leaf antiqued base. Also available in all gold or all silver leaf antiqued. Please specify, or will be shipped in combination. Shade: White textured fabric laminated over translucent vinyl with raised half round self trim bordered with gold and silver scalloped pattern matching the lamp base.
Overall Ht. 38 in.
Shade Size 16x18x20 in. deep.

No. 82A Table Lamp

Variegated gold and copper leafed ceramic base with multi-colored effect. Black teak finished sub base. Shade: White textured fabric laminated over translucent vinyl with raised half round self trim.
Overall Ht. 38 in.
Shade Size 13x16x18 in. deep.

THE TAMI COLLECTION BY MOSS

No. 85A Table Lamp

Copper leaf antiqued ceramic mounted on black base with gold leaf antiqued sub base. Shade: White textured fabric laminated over translucent vinyl, with raised self trim band combined with copper piping.
Overall Ht. 43 in.
Shade Size 14x16x20 in. deep.

No. 86A Table Lamp

Light blue pearl like finish on swirled ceramic base with antiqued gold leaf sub base. Has two gold leaf ball drops and cord as trim. Shade: White textured fabric laminated over translucent vinyl with raised self trim bordered in gold.
Overall Ht. 43 in.
Shade Size 14x16x20 in. deep.

No. 88A Table Lamp

Gold leaf antiqued in black. Available in black with green rub as 87A. Shade: White textured fabric laminated over translucent vinyl with double row of raised self trim bordering gold cord.
Overall Ht. 37 in.
Shade Size 14x16x18 in. deep.

No. 87A Table Lamp

Black ceramic base will dull green antique finish. Gold leaf antiqued sub base. Available as 88A in all gold and black. Shade: White textured fabric laminated over translucent vinyl with double row of raised self trim bordering gold cord.
Overall Ht. 37 in.
Shade Size 14x16x18 in. deep.

Page 21

PART II
"SHEDDING SOME LIGHT ON THE SUBJECT: THE MOSS INVENTORY"

CHAPTER 11
"TABLE LAMPS"

#T 744

Row one: #T 636, #T 637, #T 635, #T 679
Row two: #SR 73, #T 736, #SR 75, #T 746

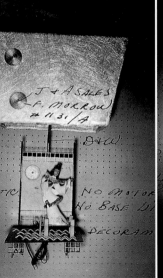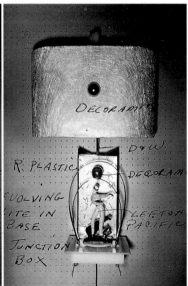

#T 715

#T 745

#T 735

#T 734, #T 733

#T 705

#T 704

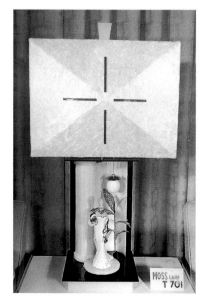

#T 701

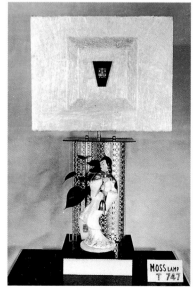

#T 747

#T 702

142

#T 717

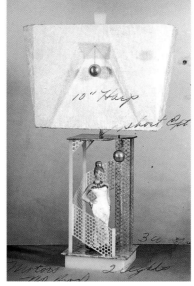

#T 683

#T 641

#T 640

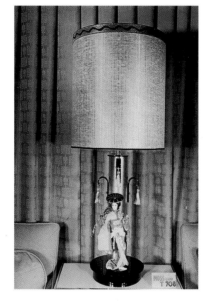

#T 708

#T 706

#SR 72

#T 714

#T 737

#T 737 variation

#T 711

#T 710

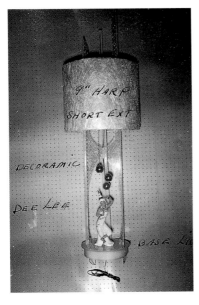

#T 622

#T 743

#T 719

#T 707

#T 709

#T 718

#T 703

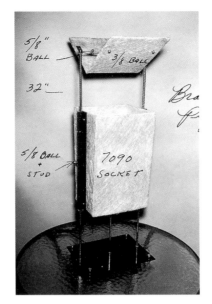

#T 616

#T 700

#T 691

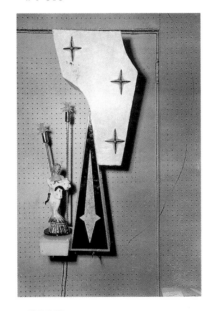

#T 568

#T 578

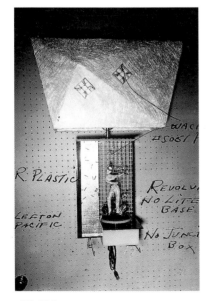

#T 634

#T 621

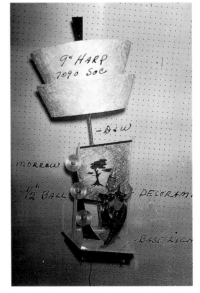

#T 623

145

#T 639

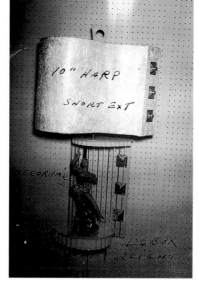

#T 620

#T 732

#T 723

#T 742

#T 713

#T 628

#T 685

#T 698

#T 697

#T 694

#T 729, #T 730

#T 695

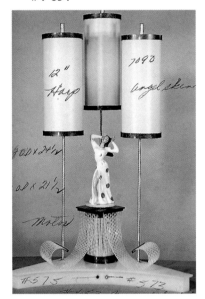

#T 680

#T 724

#T 725

#T 720

#SR 51

#T 721

#SR 5

#SR 61

#SR 62

#T 626

#T 739

#T 738

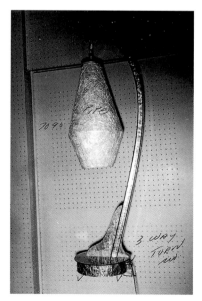

#T 646

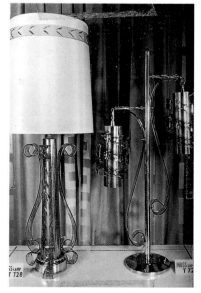

#T 728, #T 727

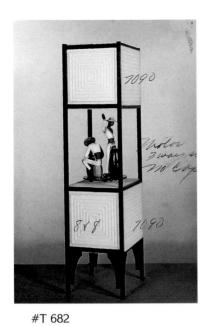

#T 682

#T 647

#SR 82

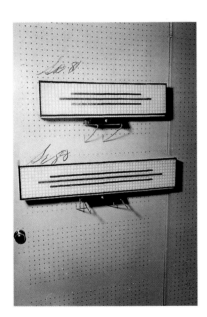

#SR 81, #SR 80

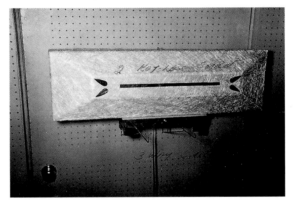

#T 649

#SR 71

#2285

#2284

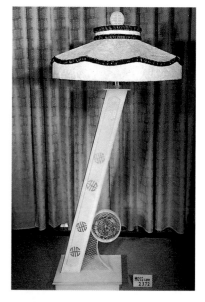

#2372

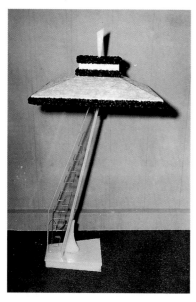

Above: #2319, **Below:** #2314 variation

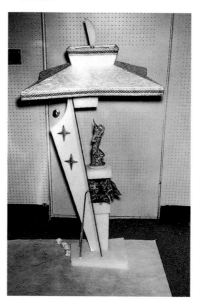

Above: #2311, **Below:** #2275

Above: #2315, **Below:** #2271

#2271 variation

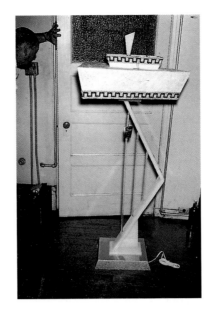

#2286

#2300

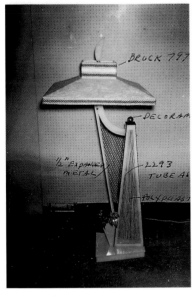

#2344

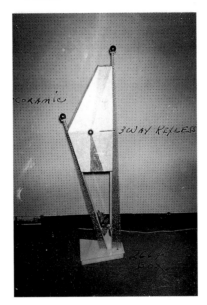

#2343

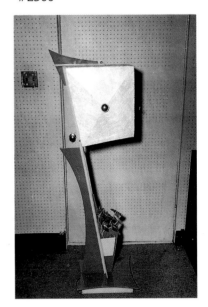

#2321

#2341

#2301 (#SR 64)

#2374

#2291

#2290

#2262

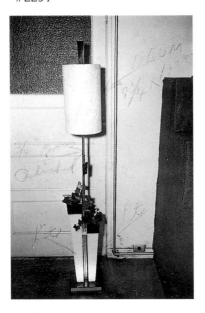

#2274

#2303

#2287

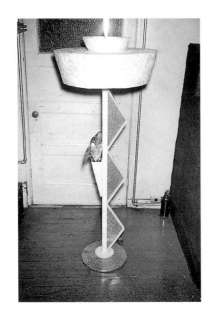

#2288

#2297

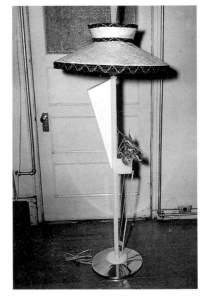

#2296

152

#2292

#SR 50

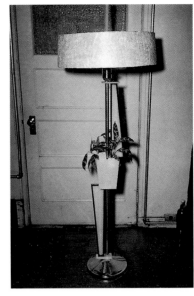

#SR 50 variation

#2292 B

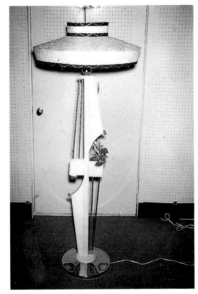

#2308

#2304

#2305

#2307

#SR 6

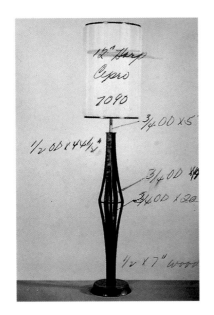

#2361

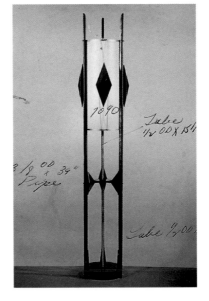

#2362

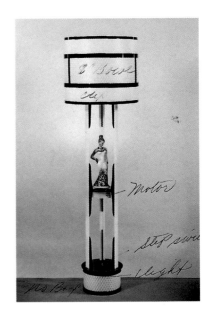

#2358

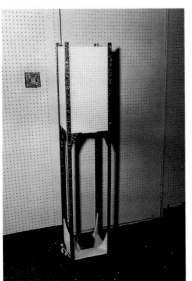

#SR 84

#2352

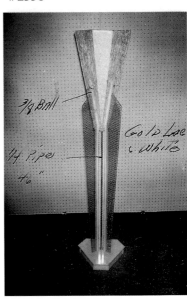

#2339

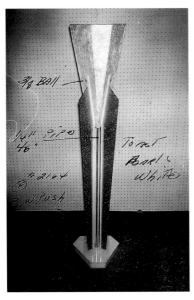

#2340

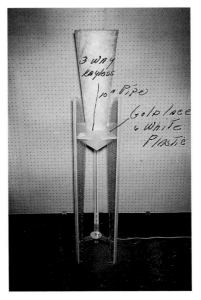

#2337

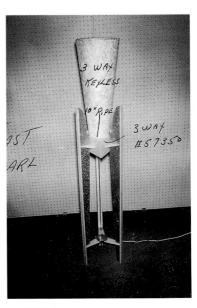

#2336

154

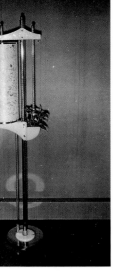

#2323

#2322

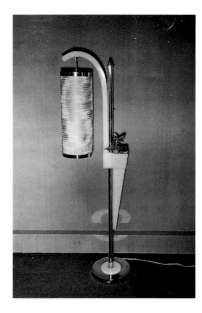

#2324

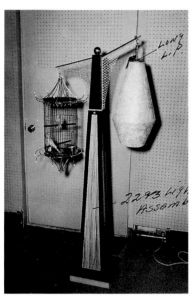

#2353

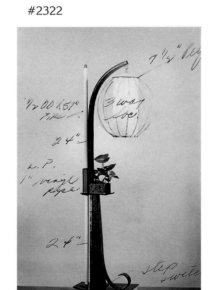

#2359

#2330

#2332

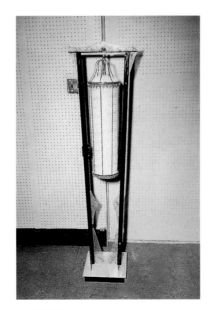

#2329

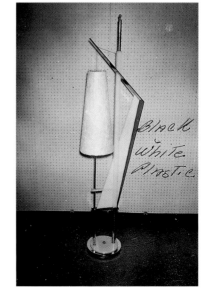

#2335

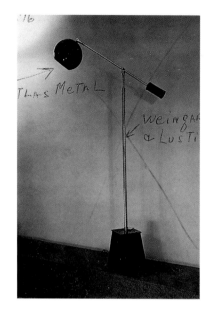

#2276

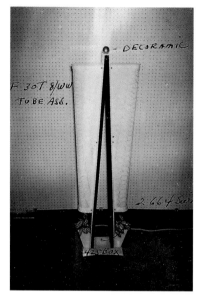

#2346

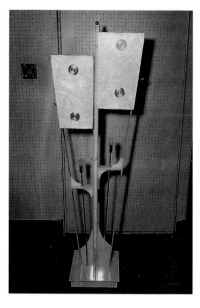

#2320

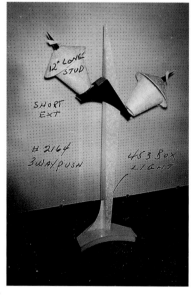

#2338

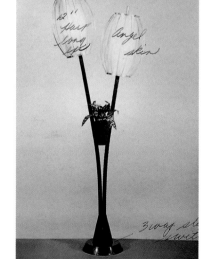

#2360

#2265

#2383

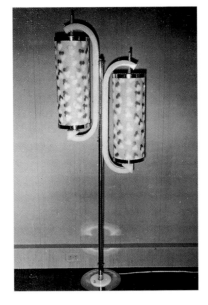

#2325

#2375

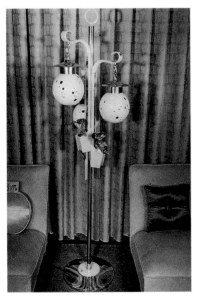

#2376

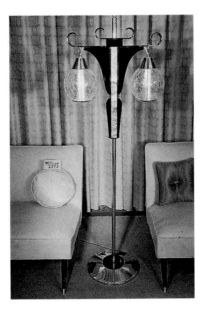

#2373

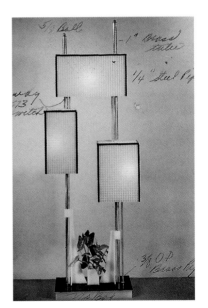

#2366

From left: #3503, #3504, #3505

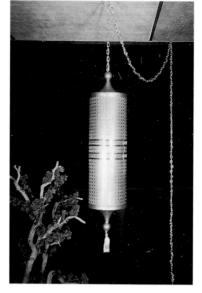

#3506

#2377

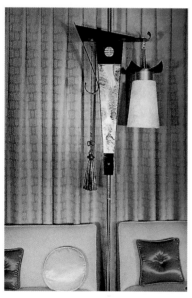

#2368

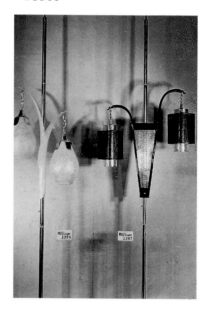

#2386 (leaf), #2387

#2370

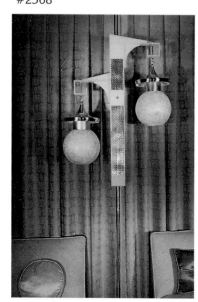

#2369

#2371

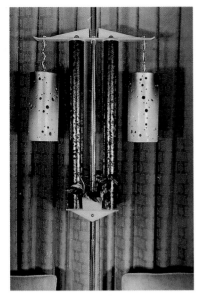

#2379

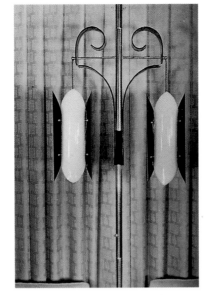

#2380

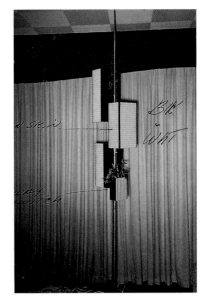

#2351

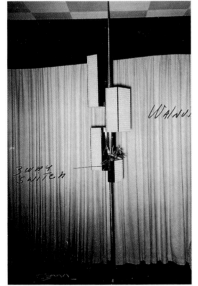

#2350

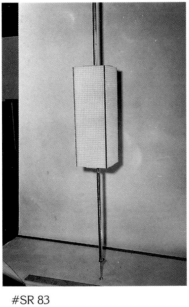

#SR 83

#2381, #2382

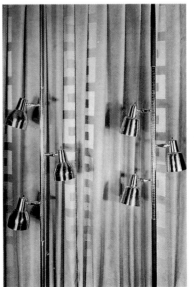

#XX 2, #XX 1

#XX 4, #XX 5 (floor)

#3002   #3000   #3001   #T 650

#3026   #3020

#T 651

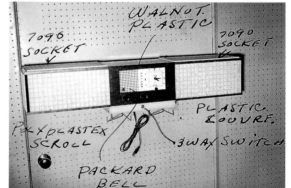

#T 648

#T 652

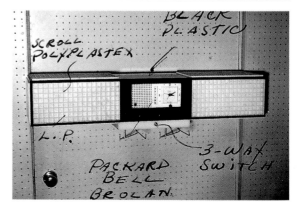

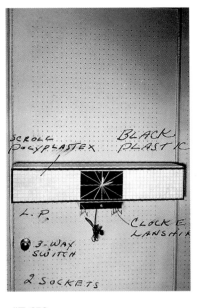

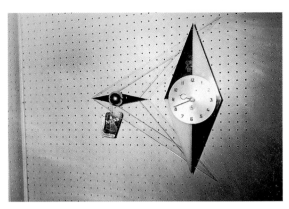

#3011

#T 653

#3009

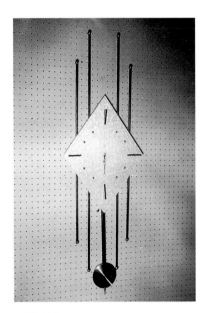

#3010

#3021

#3017

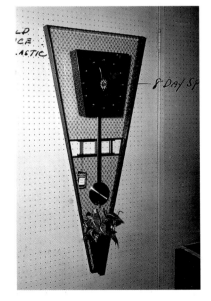

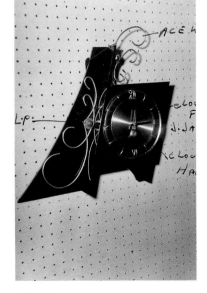

#3016

#3012

#3013

161

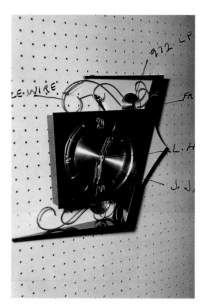

#3014

#3007

#3019

#3030

#3031

#3029

#3028

#3027

#3018

#3022

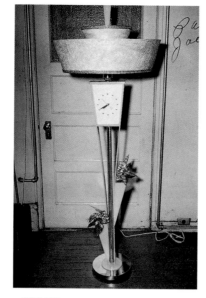

#SR 59

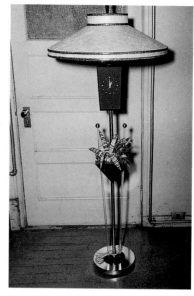

#2302

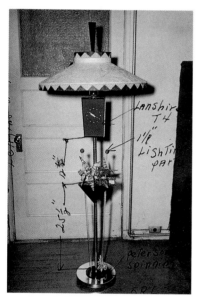

#2302 with alternate shade

#2294

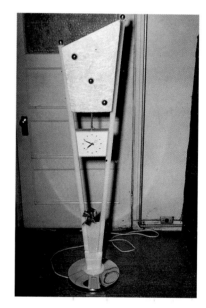

#2299

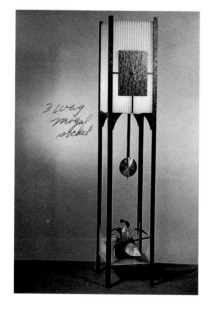

#3023

#3024

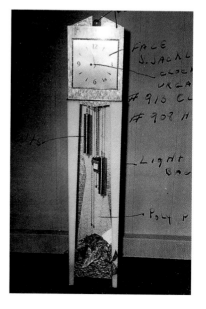

#3015

163

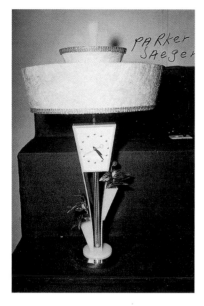

#SR 60

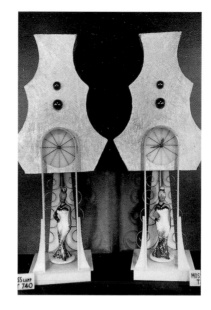

#T 740 (no clock); #T 741 (with clock)

#3008

#3004

#3003

#3005

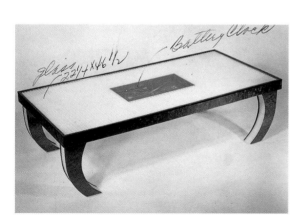

#16

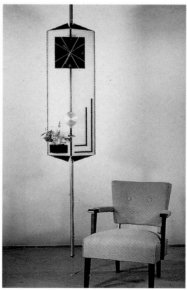

#3025

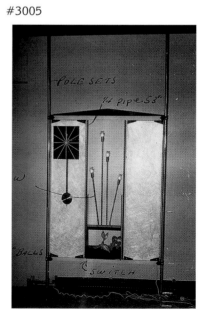

#2342

CHAPTER 15
"TABLES & BARS"

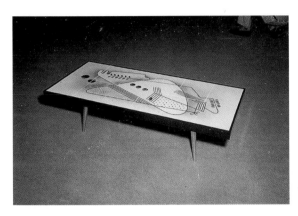

#9

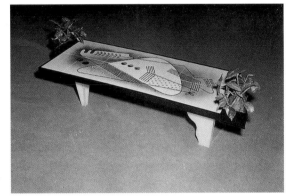

#12

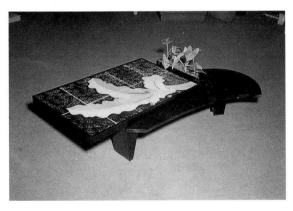

#11

#10

#13

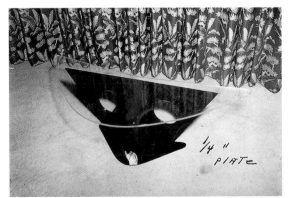

#2

#5

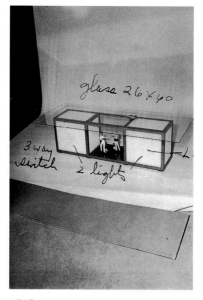

#15

#17

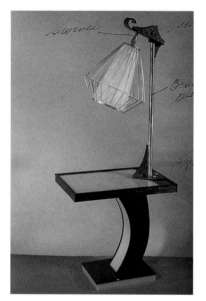

#2367

#2365

#2333

#2327

#6003

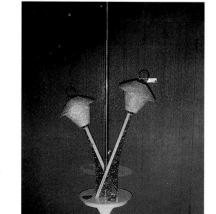

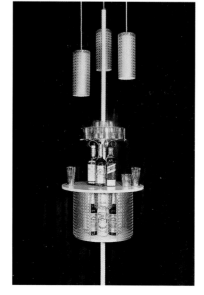

#6002

CHAPTER 16
"WALL PLAQUES & ROOM DIVIDERS"

#5011

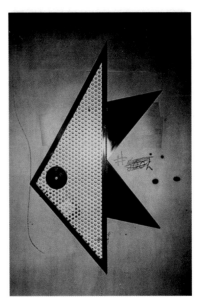

#X 5101

#5015

#5013

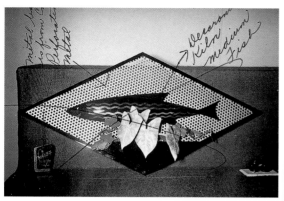

#5010

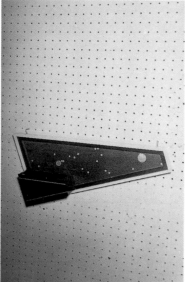

#5014

#5005

#5003

#X5102

#5004

#5008

#5009

#5012

#3500 B

#2349

#2348

#2331

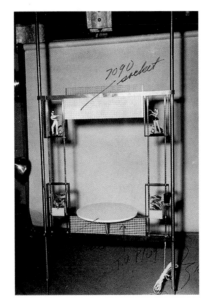

#2356

#2309

#2357

#2355

#2298

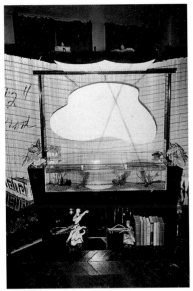

#2289

#T 693

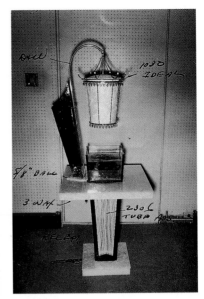

#2347

#2388, #2389 (no aquarium)

#7

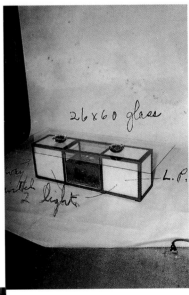

#14

#T 696

#8

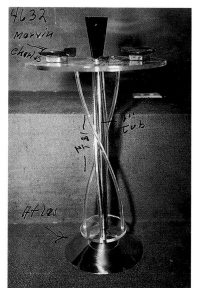

#4632

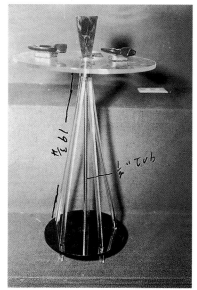

#4631

#4630

#4634

#4102 (shells),#4101 (leaves)

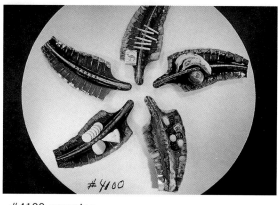

#4100 grouping

#4200 grouping

#4022 grouping

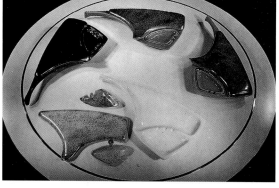

#4021 grouping

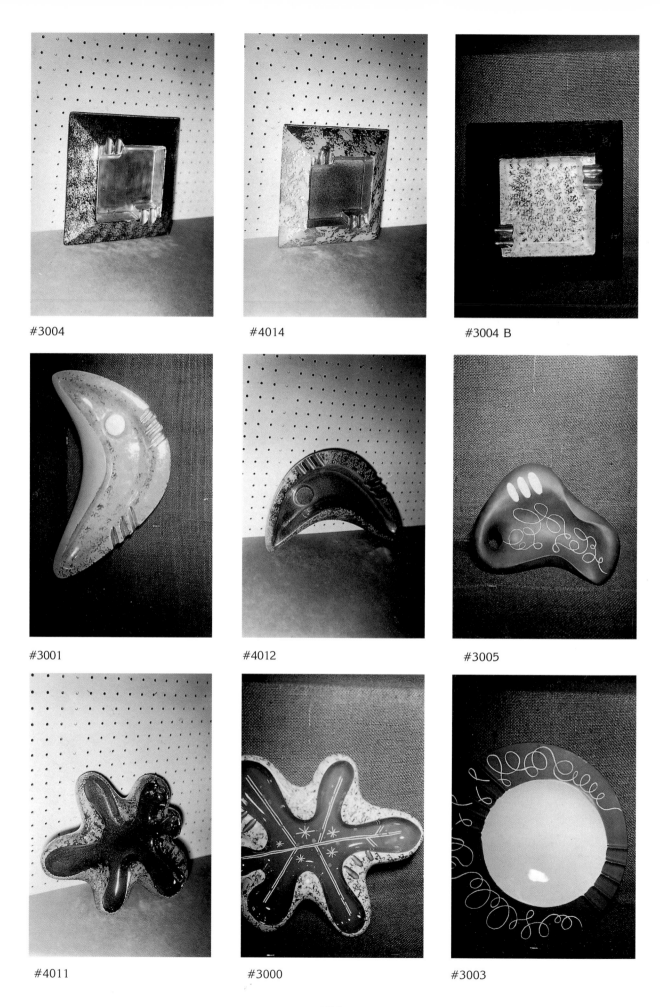

#3004

#4014

#3004 B

#3001

#4012

#3005

#4011

#3000

#3003

CHAPTER 19

"TAMI LAMPS"

#67 A

#89 A

#33 A

#59 A

#91 A

#26 A

Bottom row
left to right:
#13 A, #19 A,
#84 A

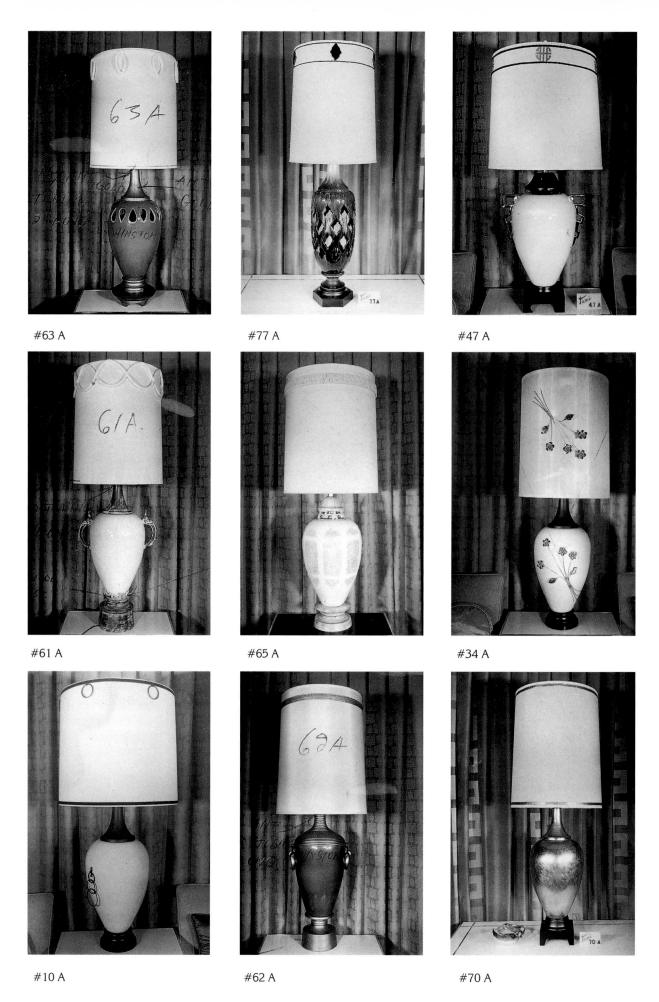

#63 A

#77 A

#47 A

#61 A

#65 A

#34 A

#10 A

#62 A

#70 A

#75 A

#40 A

#78 A

#71 A

#38 A

#57 A

#23 A

#30 A

#29 A

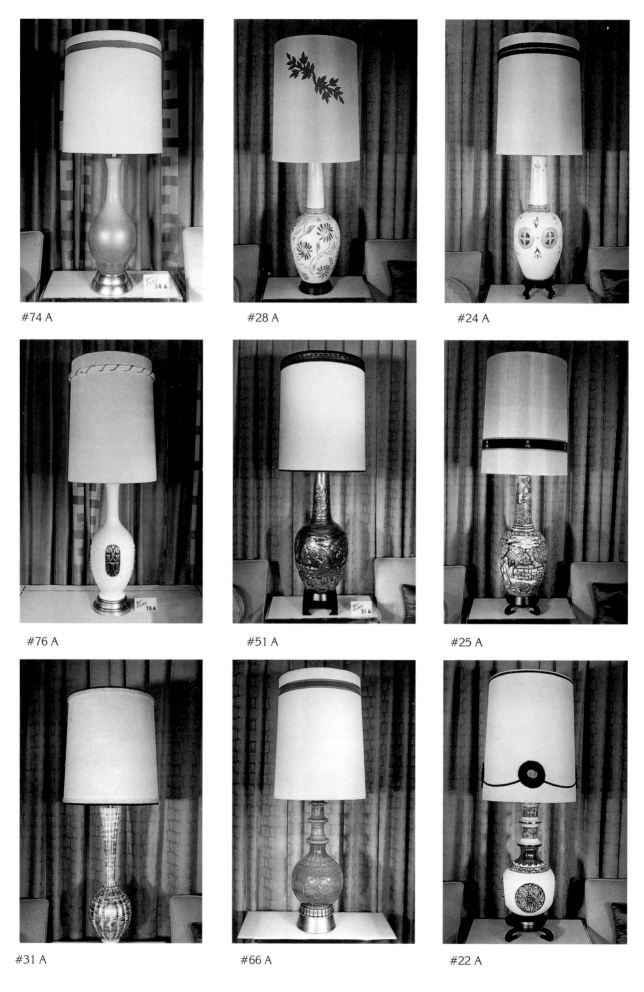

#74 A

#28 A

#24 A

#76 A

#51 A

#25 A

#31 A

#66 A

#22 A

176

#22 A variation

#49 A

#50 A

#46 A

#44 A

#42 A

#43 A

#39 A

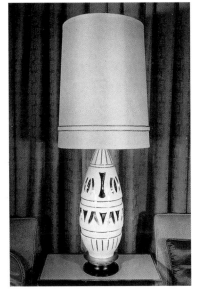

#32 A

177

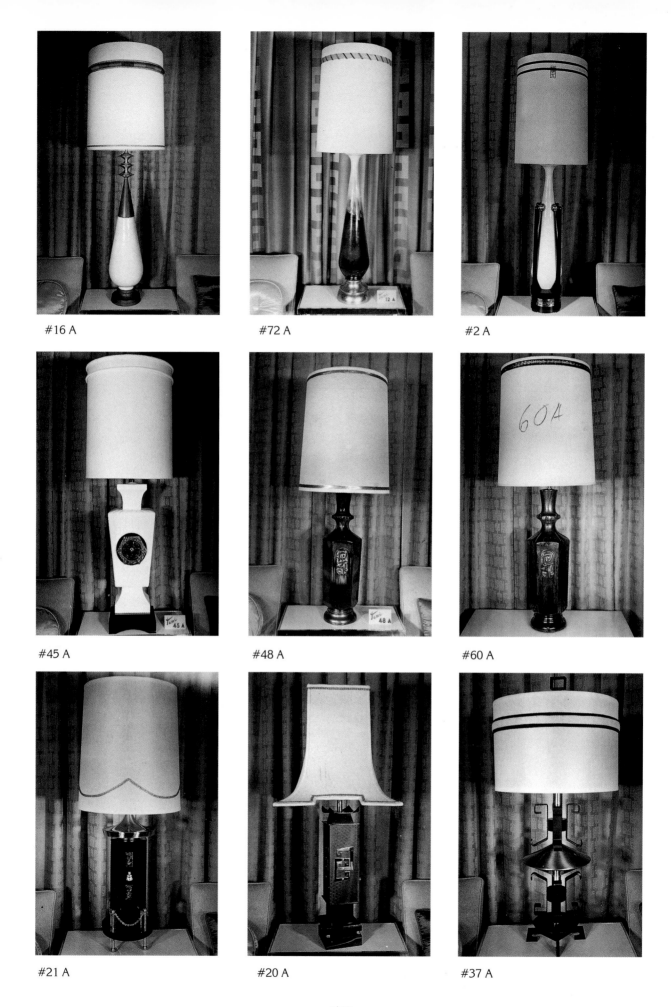

#16 A

#72 A

#2 A

#45 A

#48 A

#60 A

#21 A

#20 A

#37 A

#9 A

#7 A

#4 A

#5 A

#11 A

#8 A

#79 A

#27 A

#14 A

#41 A   #35 A   #6 A

#3 A   #36 A   #17 A

#18 A

#15 A

#64 A (pair)

#68 A, #69 A

#58 A (pair)

#80 A, #81 A

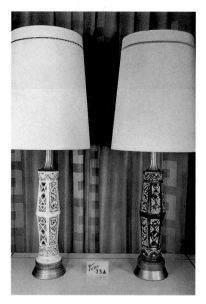

#53 A (pair)   #73 A (pair)

#82 A, #83 A   #87 A, # 88 A

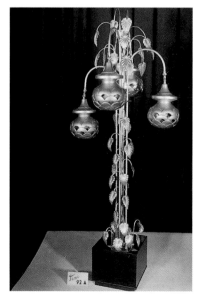

#90 A   #92 A   #93 A, #94 A

CHAPTER 20
"LIGHTS OUT: THE END OF AN ERA"

Usually, with furniture sets, we throw in a couple of lamps to close the deal. You know, buy the sofa, buy the chairs, get the lamps for free. But yesterday, I sold a Moss lamp. It's the first time I ever threw in the sofa!

Furniture salesman correspondence to Moss, mid-1950s

For nearly 20 years, Moss plexiglas lamps were just what the customer wanted. Their hefty-for-the-times price tags, (up to $80 for a table lamp, $150 for a floor model), didn't dissuade consumers looking for up-to-the-minute home decor additions. If pleasing clients by offering the Moss line meant reversing the natural order of things— throwing in the sofa instead of the lamps—enterprising furniture store owners didn't mind. A sale is a sale is a sale.

"After World War II", says longtime lamp distributor Sid Bass, "whatever you put out—people bought." Young marrieds, who had been denied the opportunity to splurge on home improvements during wartime, went on a postwar buying binge. As long as it was "new", there was a place for it. But then, as the '60s swung onward, tastes changed; what had so recently seemed ahead of the times was now running behind them. Suburban home decorating schemes of the 1960s were "unified" ones. Homemakers were encouraged to buy only those items that "went" together, from full kitchen appliance sets in lurid pastels, to complete living room suites, which included the sofa as well as the matching wall sconces above it! In this new and more selective, if not necessarily more discerning world, a plexiglas lamp was an anachronism. "When they were hot, people just loved them," says Carol Moss Goodstein, "but it's like everything else—this is such a throwaway world that we live in. One thing's out, something else is in. Still, the popularity of Moss lamps lasted a long time."

After attempting to lure back customers with increased emphasis on lamp "add-ons" (music boxes, clocks, fountains and so on), Moss faced the future by bringing out the blander, but decorator-friendly "Tami" line. Renewed interest in the Moss product was, however, only temporary. In 1968, the company stopped manufacturing altogether and became instead a distributor of European fine lamps. This, there was a market for, and "Moss Manufacturing" successfully transformed itself into "Moss Lighting". Gerry Moss died in 1992, and Moss Lighting continued under the guidance of Thelma Moss, with the company also pursuing other business interests. Finally, with Mrs. Moss' retirement in 1997, the doors closed for good on the Moss era of excitement and innovation.

Today, there's a storeroom in a Moss Properties building in San Francisco. Inside is all that remains of the past: a few boxes of lamp parts and ornaments, . . . some spun glass shades, . . . the Moss lamps rescued from Deovlet & Sons, . . . and the faithful "Shopsmith", still ready to resume work should the need ever again arise.

It probably won't, and of course it doesn't have to. The Moss heritage is unassailable. In its vast and imaginative output, Moss compiled a record of achievement that most manufacturers only dream of. The litany of Moss lamps would take even the most determined collector several lifetimes to amass. The bold unexpectedness and charm of Moss designs continues, even if only subliminally, to influence the forward-thinking designers of today. And, the determination of Thelma & Gerry Moss & Co. continues to inspire, as a true story of American success. "After all," says friend and employee Beulah Rasmussen, "lighting was their life."

Our *Stephens* is a show boat - and a GO boat, too!

says GERRY MOSS, San Francisco manufacturer, of his 51-foot Thelma IV.

"Yes, the **Thelma IV** is one of the more elaborate Stephens Cruisers," says Gerry Moss, "but, after all, she's a family hobby, so there were lots of individual demands to meet."

Stephens Brothers met the demands by combining style, speed and seaworthiness with a world of luxurious living space.

The strikingly modern interiors stem from Gerry's business. As president of the Moss Manufacturing Co., he designs and manufactures lamps, tables and cigarette lighters of plastic in contemporary and modern styling. His show-

rooms are in New York, Chicago, Buffalo, Toronto, San Francisco, Los Angeles and Honolulu.

"Extra-large water and fuel capacity allows us to cruise for weeks," Gerry explains, "and for quick trips ashore we carry an outboard-powered dingy — plus a motor scooter."

The Moss family entertains a lot, too. "Yet even with guests we're not crowded," says Thelma. "Gerry and I agree with our yachting friends that the best-built cruisers are by Stephens."

Every wheelhouse instrument is duplicated on Thelma IV's flying bridge — including the latest electronic aids. Inky, the cocker spaniel, likes cruising, too.

A Puget Sound boyhood gave Gerry Moss his love of fine boats. He is an active Coast Guard Auxiliary member, having been Commander of Flotilla II in '47, Captain of Division I in '48, and District Vice-Commodore in '49 and '50. In addition he has been Chairman of the U. S. Coast Guard Auxiliary "Over-the-Bottom" race since its inception 7 years ago, promoting it to its present national stature.

Stephens-minded Moss family includes Marilyn (Mrs. Jerome Slater), top; Carol, above, and Thelma with her husband, at left.

Stephens Cruisers ad from the early 1950s, featuring the Moss family and the *Thelma IV*. The copy notes that the cruiser's "strikingly modern interiors" stem from the "contemporary and modern styling" of Moss products.

We end as we began, with Thelma Moss, Gerry Moss, and Terry the poodle.
Were lamp sales going well? Check out the grin on Terry's face!

BIBLIOGRAPHY

Archives, Moss Manufacturing and Moss Lighting, San Francisco, CA.

Chipman, Jack. *Collector's Encyclopedia of California Pottery, Second Edition.* Paducah, KY: Collector Books, 1999.

Cope, Dwight. *Cope's Plastics Book.* South Holland, IL: The Goodheart-Willcox Co., Inc., 1973.

Cox, Susan N., ed. *20th Century American Ceramics Price Guide.* Dubuque, IA: Antique Trader Publications, 1996.

Greenberg, Cara. *Mid-Century Modern.* New York: Harmony Books, 1984, 1995.

Hine, Thomas. *Populuxe.* New York: Alfred A. Knopf, Inc., 1986.

Holthaus, Tim, and Jim Petzold, ed. *Ceramic Arts Studio Collectors Price Guide 1997.* Madison, WI: CAS Collectors Association, 1997.

Horn, Richard. *Fifties Style.* New York: Michael Friedman Publishing Group, Inc., 1993.

Jackson, Lesley. *The New Look: Design in the Fifties.* New York: Thames and Hudson Inc., 1991.

Lindenberger, Jan. *Lamps of the '50s & '60s.* Atglen, Pa: Schiffer Publishing Ltd., 1997.

"Modern Quarters." *The Echoes Report* 4, no. 2 (fall 1995): 34-36.

Payton, Leland and Crystal. *Turned On: Decorative Lamps of the 'Fifties.* New York: Abbeville Press, 1989.

Personal interviews, Moss family and employees, 1998-1999.

Personal interview, Sid Bass, 1998.

Schaefer, Joanne Fulton, and John Humphries. *deLee Art.* Butte Valley, CA: Joanne and Ralph Schaefer and John Humphries, 1997.

Steinberg, Sheila, and Kate Dooner. *Fabulous Fifties: Designs for Modern Living.* Atglen, PA: Schiffer Publishing Ltd., 1993, pp. 38-45.

Wormley, Edward J. *Dunbar Book of Modern Furniture.* Berne, IN: Dunbar Furniture Corporation, 1953.

*Learn more about the world of Moss lamps! Visit the Moss website at **http://www.mosslamps.com***

Index & Price Guide

For easy reference, all items shown in *Moss Lamps: Lighting the '50s* are listed in numerical order, by category. (A table lamp, for instance, which also includes a music box, will be found under **Music Boxes**.) Each entry gives the lamp's inventory number, followed by the page numbers(s) on which the lamp is pictured, followed by a price estimate. Prices given are for a **single** lamp or item; for pairs, simply double the value.

As with any collectible, a prime factor in determining the value of a Moss lamp is its condition. A lamp in need of extensive repair, or missing original parts, will fetch a lower price than one that is undamaged. Prices given in *Moss Lamps* are for lamps in very good condition, as defined by the following criteria:

*undamaged original shade (substitute Moss shades are also acceptable)
*plexiglas free of cracks or chips
*working motor
*unbroken figurine
*brass fittings without severe pitting or discoloration

Many Moss lamps offered for sale may, of course, fail to pass muster in one or more of these areas. However, if the sale price takes any such damage into account, the lamp may still be a worthwhile investment. (As Chapter 6 discusses in detail, even the most horrendous damage is often repairable!)

Minus factors

As noted, the asking price for a Moss lamp should reflect its condition. The deficiencies listed below will affect a lamp's value in the approximate percentages noted, using the values given in this Guide as a starting point:

*non-Moss shade (subtract 15%)
*non-working motor (subtract 25%)
*plexiglas/figural damage (subtract 50%)

Plus factors

As the prices in this Guide indicate, you can always expect to pay more for the following:

*items such as bars, or lamps with waterworks, which were not produced in great quantities, and are thus more difficult to find.
*lamps with special features, such as music boxes or clocks
*lamps featuring figurines by "name" design firms such as Hedi Schoop or Ceramic Arts Studio. In these cases the value of the figurine itself has been added to the basic lamp value. (See Chapter 3 for additional information on figurine values.)
*lamps with plexiglas in less common colors, such as pink or blue.

The value of a Value Guide

The values in *Moss Lamps* have been determined after consultation with collectors and dealers who specialize in lamps of the 1950s. Their input has been combined with current auction and sale prices for Moss lamps, as well as our knowledge of product availability. The estimates given are reasonable averages based on this information. Please keep in mind, however, that an estimate is only an estimate; any price guide is best viewed as a tool to assist you in beginning negotiations. Prices will always vary from dealer to dealer, and may be different in different parts of the country. The authors cannot guarantee that you will be able to purchase a Moss lamp at the prices shown. We do, however, guarantee that you will enjoy the search—and that ownership of a Moss lamp will definitely "light up your life!"

Table Lamps

SR 5—p. 148—$100-125
SR 51—p. 147—$100-125
SR 61—p. 148—$100-125
SR 62—p. 148—$125-150
SR 71—p. 149—$125-150
SR 72—p. 143—$125-150
SR 73—pp. 33, 141—$200-225
SR 74—p. 29—$175-200
SR 75—p. 141—$175-200
SR 80—p. 149—$75-100
SR 81—p. 149—$75-100
SR 82—p. 149—$100-125
T 459—pp. 107, 119—$125-150
T 474—p. 119—$125-150
T 476—pp. 40, 91, 120—$200-225
T 543—pp. 32, 68, 120—$200-225
T 544—pp. 100, 120—$300-325
T 568—p. 145—$375-400
T 569—p. 107—$225-250
T 578—pp. 121, 145—$175-200
T 579—pp. 30, 68, 121—$300-325
T 616—p. 145—$125-150
T 617—pp. 34, 97, 121—$200-225
T 620—p. 146—$175-200
T 621—p. 145—$175-200
T 622—p. 144—$200-225
T 623—p. 145—$200-225
T 626—p. 148—$125-150
T 628—p. 146—$175-200
T 632—p. 30—$175-200
T 633—pp. 95, 122—$150-175
T 634—pp. 122, 145—$200-225
T 635—pp. 122, 141—$200-225
T 636—p. 141—$150-175
T 637—p. 141—$200-225
T 638—p. 95—$150-175
T 639—p. 146—$175-200
T 640—p. 143—$200-225
T 641—p. 143—$175-200
T 646—p. 148—$150-175
T 647—p. 149—$100-125
T 649—p. 149—$100-125
T 679—p. 141—$200-225
T 680—p. 147—$300-325
T 681—p. 35—$300-325
T 682—p. 149—$200-225
T 683—p. 143—$175-200
T 685—p. 146—$175-200
T 687—p. 19—$125-150
T 690—pp. 84, 124—$175-200
T 691—p. 145—$225-250
T 694—p. 147—$175-200
T 695—p. 147—$175-200
T 697—p. 147—$175-200
T 698—pp. 124, 146—$200-225
T 700—pp. 124, 145—$175-200
T 701—p. 142—$175-200
T 702—p. 142—$200-225
T 703—p. 145—$125-150
T 704—p. 142—$200-225
T 705—p. 142—$200-225
T 706—p. 143—$175-200
T 707—p. 144—$175-200
T 708—p. 143—$200-225
T 709—p. 144—$175-200

T 710—p. 144—$200-225
T 711—p. 144—$175-200
T 712—pp. 99, 124—$350-375
T 713—pp. 125, 146—$175-200
T 714—p. 143—$200-225
T 715—pp. 125, 142—$175-200
T 716—pp. 80, 125—$200-225
T 717—p. 143—$175-200
T 718—p. 144—$175-200
T 719—p. 144—$200-225
T 720—p. 147—$100-125
T 721—p. 148—$100-125
T 722—p. 81—$175-200
T 723—p. 146—$200-225
T 724—p. 147—$200-225
T 725—pp. 118, 147—$200-225
T 727—pp. 125, 148—$125-150
T 728—pp. 125, 148—$125-150
T 729—p. 147—$150-175
T 730—p. 147—$150-175
T 731—pp. 4, 34, 94, 126—$300-325
T 732—pp. 126, 146—$175-200
T 733—pp. 126, 142—$175-200
T 734—pp. 126, 142—$175-200
T 735—pp. 126, 142—$150-175
T 736—pp. 127, 141—$175-200
T 737—pp. 127, 143, 144—$200-225
T 738—pp. 127, 148—$150-175
T 739—pp. 127, 148—$150-175
T 740—pp. 23, 84, 128, 164—$175-200
T 742—pp. 128, 146—$200-225
T 743—pp. 128, 144—$175-200
T 744—pp. 128, 141—$175-200
T 745—pp. 129, 142—$175-200
T 746—pp. 129, 141—$175-200
T 747—pp. 129, 142—$175-200
XT 800—p. 13—$125-150
XT 801—p. 29—$175-200
XT 802—p. 31—$175-200
XT 803—pp. 32, 90—$200-225
XT 804—p. 33—$175-200
XT 805—p. 36—$175-200
XT 806—p. 37—$275-300
XT 807—pp. 1, 38, 87, back cover—$250-275
XT 808—pp. 39, 84—$250-275
XT 809—p. 41—$350-375
XT 810—p. 35—$225-250
XT 811—p. 35—$200-225
XT 812—p. 42—$200-225
XT 813—pp. 39, 81—$250-275
XT 814—p. 68—$175-200
XT 816—p. 79—$200-225
XT 817—p. 117—$125-150
XT 818—p. 81—$125-150
XT 819—p. 82—$225-250
XT 820—p. 82—$175-200
XT 821—p. 83—$200-225
XT 822—p. 85—$275-300
XT 823—p. 85—$200-225
XT 824—p. 85—$200-225
XT 825—p. 86—$150-175
XT 826—p. 86—$125-150
XT 827—p. 88—$375-400
XT 828—p. 89—$125-150
XT 829—p. 90—$150-175
XT 830—p. 90—$175-200
XT 831—p. 92—$150-175 Decoramic; $200-225 Yona
XT 832—p. 103—$125-150

XT 833—p. 96—$150-175
XT 834—p. 96—$200-225
XT 835—p. 98—$125-150
XT 836—p. 101—$300-325
XT 837—pp. 2, 101—$300-325
XT 838—p. 102—$325-350
XT 839—p. 103—$150-175
XT 840—p. 103—$225-250
XT 841—p. 104—$100-125
XT 842—p. 105—$100-125
XT 843—p. 105—$175-200
XT 844—p. 105—$125-150
XT 845—p. 106—$100-125
XT 846—p. 106—$200-225
XT 847—p. 107—$200-225
XT 854—p. 89—$150-175
XT 856—p. 41—$950-1000
XT 857—p. 99—$225-250
XT 859—p. 40—$350-375

FLOOR LAMPS

XX 5—p. 159—$50-75
SR 6—p. 153—$175-200
SR 50—p. 153—$175-200
SR 84—p. 154—$175-200
2235—p. 19—$200-225
2249—p. 111—$375-400
2262—p. 152—$200-225
2265—p. 156—$350-375
2271—pp. 150, 151—$225-250
2273—p. 78—$200-225
2274—p. 152—$200-225
2275—p. 150—$225-250
2276—p. 156—$275-300
2278—p. 78—$175-200
2284—pp. 129, 150—$250-275
2285—pp. 130, 150—$250-275
2286—p. 151—$225-250
2287—p. 152—$175-200
2288—p. 152—$175-200
2290—p. 152—$200-225
2291—p. 152—$200-225
2292—p. 153—$175-200
2292 B—p. 153—$175-200
2293—pp. 23, 108, 109, 130—$275-300
2295—pp. 76, 114, 130—$250-275
2296—p. 152—$175-200
2297—p. 152—$175-200
2300—p. 151—$225-250
2301/SR 64—p. 151—$200-225
2303—p. 152—$175-200
2304—p. 153—$175-200
2305—p. 153—$175-200
2306—p. 110—$225-250
2307—p. 153—$175-200
2308—p. 153—$175-200
2310—pp. 7, 73, 111—$450-475
2311—p. 150—$425-450
2312—p. 113—$300-325
2314—pp. 112, 150—$325-350
2315—p. 150—$425-450
2316—p. 31—$475-500
2317—pp. 30, 110, front cover—$600-625
2318—p. 116—$525-550
2319—p. 150—$175-200
2320—p. 156—$300-325

2321—p. 151—$300-325
2322—p. 155—$250-275
2323—p. 155—$250-275
2324—p. 155—$250-275
2325—p. 157—$200-225
2328—p. 117—$400-425
2329—p. 155—$500-525
2330—p. 155—$525-550
2332—p. 155—$525-550
2334—p. 115—$500-525
2335—p. 155—$500-525
2336—p. 154—$200-225
2337—p. 154—$200-225
2338—p. 156—$300-325
2339—p. 154—$200-225
2340—p. 154—$200-225
2341—p. 151—$225-250
2343—p. 151—$300-325
2344—p. 151—$275-300
2345—p. 112—$475-500
2346—p. 156—$275-300
2352—p. 154—$175-200
2353—p. 155—$525-550
2354—pp. 113, 131—$475-500
2358—p. 154—$475-500
2359—p. 155—$500-525
2360—p. 156—$300-325
2361—p. 154—$175-200
2362—p. 154—$200-225
2366—p. 157—$275-300
2372—p. 150—$200-225
2373—pp. 132, 157—$250-275
2374—p. 151—$200-225
2375—p. 157—$275-300
2376—pp. 132, 157—$250-275
2383—pp. 133, 157—$225-250
X 2400—p. 13—$225-250
X 2401—pp. 72, 113—$250-275
X 2402—p. 78—$175-200
X 2403—p. 78—$175-200
X 2404—p. 69—$525-550
X 2405—p. 113—$375-400
X 2406—p. 114—$175-200
X 2407—p. 117—$250-275

HANGING LAMPS

3500—p. 53—$175-200
3503—p. 158—$175-200
3504—p. 158—$175-200
3505—p. 158—$175-200
3506—p. 158—$175-200

FLOOR-TO-CEILING LAMPS

XX 1—p. 159—$75-100
XX 2—p. 159—$75-100
XX 4—p. 159—$75-100
SR 83—p. 159—$175-200
2350—p. 159—$425-450
2351—p. 159—$425-450
2368—p. 158—$425-450
2369—pp. 131, 158—$425-450
2370—pp. 131, 158—$425-450
2371—pp. 132, 158—$425-450
2377—pp. 132, 158—$750-800

2378—p. 45—$750-800
2379—pp. 133, 159—$425-450
2380—p. 159—$425-450
2381—pp. 133, 159—$425-450
2382—pp. 133, 159—$425-450
2387—pp. 133, 158—$425-450
2389—p. 170—$425-450

Clock Lamps

16—p. 164—$725-750
SR 59—p. 163—$275-300
SR 60—p. 164—$150-175
T 648—p. 160—$175-200
T 650—p. 160—$175-200
T 651—p. 160—$175-200
T 652—p. 160—$175-200
T 653—p. 161—$175-200
T 741—pp. 128, 164—$275-300
XT 815—pp. 55, 72—$275-300; p. 56 (no clock)—$200-225
2294—p. 163—$275-300
2299—p. 163—$275-300
2302—p. 163—$275-300
2342—p. 164—$1000-1200
3000—p. 160—$75-100
3001—p. 160—$100-125
3002—p. 160—$75-100
3003—p. 164—$250-275
3004—p. 164—$175-200
3005—p. 164—$175-200
3006—p. 55—$175-200
3007—p. 162—$325-350
3008—p. 164—$275-300
3009—p. 161—$175-200
3010—p. 161—$175-200
3011—p. 161—$175-200
3012—p. 161—$175-200
3013—p. 161—$175-200
3014—p. 162—$175-200
3015—p. 163—$400-425
3016—p. 161—$325-350
3017—p. 161—$200-225
3018—pp. 134, 162—$250-275
3019—p. 162—$250-275
3020—p. 160—$200-225
3021—p. 161—$200-225
3022—p. 163—$750-800
3023—p. 163—$350-375
3024—p. 163—$350-375
3025—p. 164—$500-525
3026—pp. 134, 160—$200-225
3027—p. 162—$250-275
3028—pp. 134, 162—$250-275
3029—pp. 134, 162—$250-275
3030—pp. 135, 162—$250-275
3031—pp. 135, 162—$250-275
X 3100—p. 77—$350-375
X 3101—p. 56—$150-175
X 3102—p. 55—$75-100

Tables

2—p. 165—$625-650
5—p. 166—$625-650
9—p. 165—$650-675
10—p. 165—$675-700
11—p. 165—$675-700

12—p. 165—$675-700
13—p. 165—$675-700
15—p. 166—$675-700
17—pp. 59, 166—$725-750
2327—p. 166—$725-750
2333—p. 166—$700-725
2365—p. 166—$725-750
2367—p. 166—$725-750

Bars

6000—p. 59—$2000-2200
6001—p. 59—$2400-2500
6002—p. 166—$2300-2400
6003—p. 166—$2000-2200

Wall Plaques

5000—p. 37—$400-450
5001—p. 37—$350-400
5002—p. 60—$350-400
5003—p. 168—$500-550
5004—p. 168—$500-550
5005—p. 168—$300-350
5006—p. 41—$500-550
5007—p. 42—$300-350
5008—p. 168—$300-350
5009—p. 168—$300-350
5010—p. 168—$250-300
5011—p. 167—$125-175
5012—p. 168—$500-550
5013—p. 167—$125-175
5014—p. 168—$125-175
5015—p. 167—$175-225
X 5100—p. 77—$450-500
X 5101—p. 167—$125-175
X 5102—p. 168—$300-350

Room Dividers

2272—p. 60—$750-1000
2298—p. 169—$750-1000
2309—p. 169—$750-1000
2331—p. 169—$1000-1200
2348—p. 169—$750-1000
2349—p. 169—$750-1000
2355—p. 169—$1000-1200
2356—p. 169—$1000-1200
2357—p. 169—$1000-1200
3500 B—p. 169—$500-750
3501—p. 42—$500-750

Waterworks

1—pp. 58, 121—$700-800
6—p. 42—$900-1000
7—pp. 122, 170—$600-700
8—p. 170—$500-600
14—p. 170—$300-400
T 693—p. 170—$800-900
T 696—p. 170—$1200-1300
T 699—pp. 26, 57—$1100-1200
T 726—p. 58—$1200-1300
XT 853—p. 57—$1200-1300
XT 858—p. 58—$400-500

2289—p. 170—$1300-1400
2347—p. 170—$900-1000
2388—p. 170—$600-700

MUSIC BOX LAMPS

T 534—pp. 36, 50, 51, 120—$275-300
T 666—pp. 52, 123—$250-275
T 667—pp. 52, 123—$250-275
T 684—pp. 52, 123—$250-275
XT 848—p. 50—$250-275
XT 849—p. 52—$275-300
XT 855—p. 33—$275-300

INTERCOM LAMPS

T 627—p. 53—$375-400

"REVOLVE" LAMPS

T 686—p. 53—$400-425
T 689—p. 53—$375-400
2364—p. 53—$375-400
3501—p. 53—$250-275
3502—p. 53—$250-275

"SPINNER" LAMPS

XT 850—p. 54—$275-300

TV LAMPS

XT 851—p. 54—$150-175

RADIO LAMPS

XT 852—p. 54—$350-375

"LEAF" LAMPS

SR 52—p. 48—$75-100
T 688—pp. 47, 123—$75-100
2250—p. 48—$175-200
2277—p. 49—$200-225
2326—pp. 49, 130—$225-250
2363—pp. 49, 131—$175-200
2386—pp. 133, 158—$425-450
4629—p. 49—$225-250

SMOKESTANDS

4630—p. 171—$200-225
4631—p. 171—$200-225
4632—p. 171—$200-225
4633—p. 43—$200-225
4634—p. 171—$225-250
4635—p. 35—$225-250

ASHTRAYS

3000—p. 172—$35-40
3001—p. 172—$25-30

3002—p. 43—$25-30
3003—p. 172—$35-40
3004—p. 172—$25-30
3004 B—p. 172—$25-30
3005—p. 172—$35-40
3006—p. 43—$35-40
4011—p. 172—$35-40
4012—p. 172—$25-30
4013—p. 43—$25-30
4014—p. 172—$25-30
4019—p. 43—$40-45
4020—p. 43—$45-50
4021—p. 171—$25-30
4022—p. 171—$25-30
4100—p. 171—$25-30
4101—p. 171—$25-30
4102—p. 171—$25-30
4200—p. 171—$25-30

TAMI LAMPS

2 A—p. 178—$50-75
3 A—p. 180—$75-100
4 A—p. 179—$75-100
5 A—p. 179—$75-100
6 A—p. 180—$75-100
7 A—p. 179—$75-100
8 A—p. 179—$75-100
9 A—p. 179—$100-125
10 A—p. 174—$50-75
11 A—pp. 135, 179—$75-100
13 A—p. 173—$75-100
14 A—p. 179—$75-100
15 A—p. 181—$75-100
16 A—p. 178—$50-75
17 A—p. 180—$75-100
18 A—p. 181—$75-100
19 A—pp. 135, 173—$75-100
20 A—p. 178—$75-100
21 A—p. 178—$75-100
22 A—pp. 176, 177—$50-75
23 A—p. 175—$50-75
24 A—p. 176—$50-75
25 A—p. 176—$50-75
26 A—p. 173—$75-100
27 A—p. 179—$75-100
28 A—p. 176—$75-100
29 A—p. 175—$50-75
30 A—p. 175—$50-75
31 A—p. 176—$50-75
32 A—p. 177—$50-75
33 A—p. 173—$100-125
34 A—pp. 136, 174—$75-100
35 A—p. 180—$100-125
36 A—p. 180—$75-100
37 A—p. 178—$75-100
38 A—p. 175—$50-75
39 A—p. 177—$50-75
40 A—p. 175—$50-75
41 A—p. 180—$75-100
42 A—p. 177—$50-75
43 A—p. 177—$50-75
44 A—p. 177—$50-75
45 A—p. 178—$50-75
46 A—p. 177—$50-75
47 A—p. 174—$50-75
48 A—p. 178—$50-75
49 A—p. 177—$50-75

50 A—pp. 136, 177—$50-75
51 A—p. 176—$50-75
52 A—p. 47—$100-125
53 A—p. 182—$50-75
55 A—pp. 46, 136—$50-75
56 A—p. 136—$50-75
57 A—pp. 137, 175—$50-75
58 A—p. 181—$50-75
59 A—p. 173—$100-125
60 A—p. 178—$50-75
61 A—pp. 137, 174—$50-75
62 A—p. 174—$50-75
63 A—p. 174—$50-75
64 A—pp. 137, 181—$50-75
65 A—p. 174—$50-75
66 A—p. 176—$50-75
67 A—p. 173—$100-125
68 A—pp. 137, 181—$50-75
69 A—pp. 137, 181—$50-75
70 A—pp. 138, 174—$50-75
71 A—pp. 138, 175—$50-75
72 A—pp. 138, 178—$50-75

73 A—p. 182—$50-75
74 A—pp. 46, 138, 176—$50-75
75 A—pp. 139, 175—$50-75
76 A—pp. 139, 176—$50-75
77 A—pp. 46, 174—$50-75
78 A—p. 175—$50-75
79 A—pp. 139, 179—$50-75
80 A—pp. 139, 181—$50-75
81 A—pp. 139, 181—$50-75
82 A—pp. 140, 182—$50-75
83 A—pp. 140, 182—$50-75
84 A—pp. 140, 173—$50-75
85 A—pp. 46, 140—$50-75
86 A—pp. 46, 140—$50-75
87 A—pp. 140, 182—$50-75
88 A—pp. 140, 182—$50-75
89 A—p. 173—$100-125
90 A—p. 182—$100-125
91 A—p. 173—$100-125
92 A—p. 182—$100-125
93 A—p. 182—$100-125
94 A—p. 182—$100-125

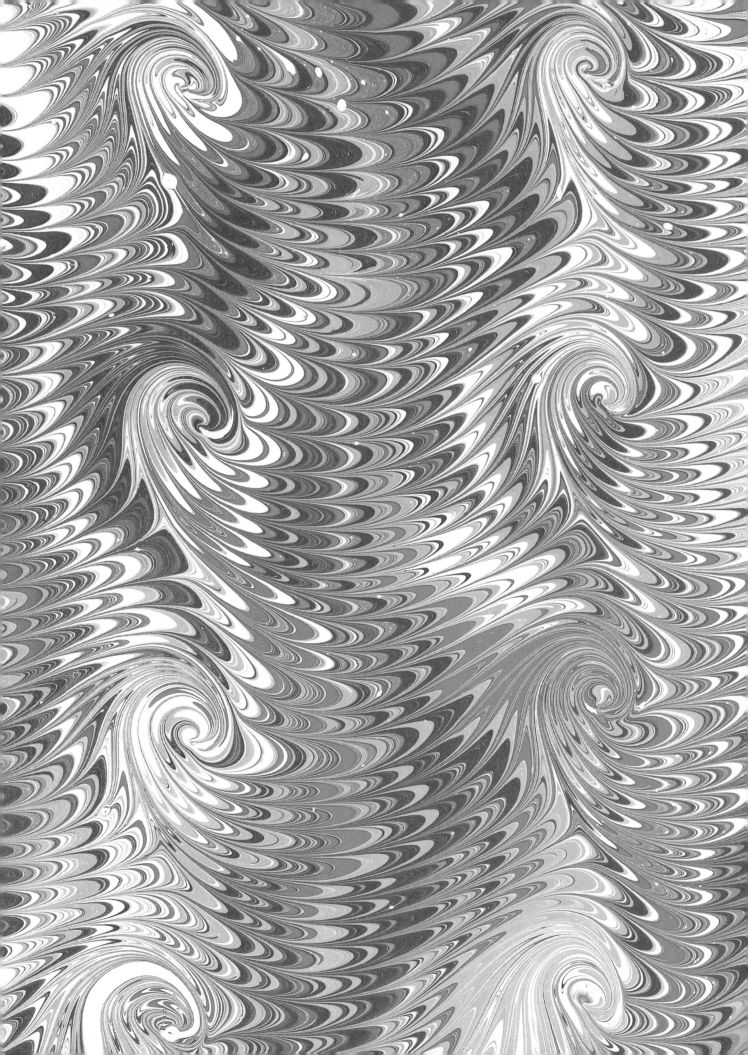